Made for a Mission

Made for a Mission

David A. Posthuma

PUBLICATIONS

Fort Washington, PA 19034

Made for a Mission

Published by CLC Publications

U.S.A.
P.O. Box 1449, Fort Washington, PA 19034

GREAT BRITAIN
51 The Dean, Alresford, Hants. SO24 9BJ

AUSTRALIA
P.O. Box 2299, Strathpine, QLD 4500

NEW ZEALAND
10 MacArthur Street, Feilding

ISBN   978-0-87508-981-2

Printed in the United States of America

Dedication

This book is dedicated to my children, Alyssa and Joshua. It is my prayer that each of you would seek first the kingdom of God, and in so doing, realize that God intentionally created you to be a princess and prince within His kingdom. God knew each of you even before He created you and instilled within you incredible gifts and abilities to be used in His service. It is my honor to be your father and to help you discover the mission God has in store for your life. Always remember that I love you with an unfailing love but that my love pales in comparison with Christ's love for you. Rely always upon His love, and may His love compel you to accomplish great things for Christ's kingdom.

Contents

Introduction

Every Saturday night in the 1970s I sat glued to our black-and-white television watching *Mission Impossible*. I reveled in the fantasy of receiving a secret mission that would require me to risk everything to overcome the "bad guys." Little did I realize then that my fantasy would become reality when I came to Christ.

In the heart of every Christ-follower is a tape-recorded message which reveals his or her life mission, but unlike the message on *Mission Impossible*, it does not self-destruct after ten seconds. It may get lost in the noise and apathy of daily life, but it is always there—seeking to be heard, seeking to be obeyed. Each one of us is called to complete our unique role in the Great Commission, a mission which comes directly from our God and Creator. His "call" is recorded on each of our hearts, and we can hear it if we rightly attune our mind, emotions and spirit.

Have you ever listened—really listened—to your heart? It can tell you much about your divine mission in this world. Each one of us has a unique "heart's cry" that helps us discern the reason for which we were created. It is the emotive force given to us by our Creator which drives us to discover and fulfill our ordained mission. Understanding that mission can be a complex and confusing process. In fact, seeking to discover your mission is probably why you are now reading this book. The first step in this discovery process is to respond to the cry of your heart.

Consider for a moment the word "mission." What feelings does that word evoke within you? What picture forms in your mind? A man or woman "on a mission" is consumed with a particular objective. It is nothing less than the dominant priority of life. Make no mistake: This book is not about mere volunteerism. Your ministry mission—God's call upon your life—cannot simply be another layer added to an already busy schedule. Hearing and responding to God's call will inevitably transform your life. It will generate a profound desire to re-orient your family, finances and priorities to better accommodate the mission God has ordained for you.

> A "heart's cry" is the emotive force given to us by our Creator which drives us to discover and fulfill our ordainded mission in this world.

A true mission will be multi-faceted, consisting of various developmental phases over the different stages of life, with layers of intersecting priorities. However, if God is leading you to achieve your ultimate life mission, these phases and priorities will not lead you away from His ultimate goal for you. Instead they will converge over time, enabling you to become a highly effective servant in Christ's kingdom.

For years I was confused about my mission in this world. God had given me two seemingly incongruent passions: technology and pastoral ministry. I had an innate interest in technology and had created technological systems and solutions from my earliest childhood. When I became a committed Christ-follower, I also developed a deep passion for helping others grow spiritually. I did not understand how these two passions fit together, so I chose what I believed to be the noble path: I suppressed my passion for technology and pursued ministry.

I soon learned that because I was entrepreneurial and creative, I thrived in ministry ventures in which I was able to develop new systems, churches and programs. It was this same passion that inspired me to support the spiritual formation process in the lives of others. I discovered a truth about myself that I had always known but had never dreamed would apply in a ministry context: I was a "builder." I had to build. I could not help myself.

The passion to build programs, churches, systems and structures had been ordained in my inmost being by God, who saw me in His mind's eye before He laid the foundations of the earth (Proverbs 8:22–31). My desire to help believers lay a healthy spiritual foundation and grow to maturity was simply one expression of my "builder" passion. I found that when I was building, I was physically energized, spiritually vitalized and emotionally satisfied. Whenever I was no longer able to build, my stress level skyrocketed and my satisfaction level hit an all-time low.

I encountered these highs and lows during my first church-planting venture. Initially I found the church-planting process very fulfilling. God gave me a small core of twelve people, and within a year we had grown to a congregation of 135, with no signs of slowing.

Satan, however, had other plans; he used pride to fracture our leadership. Only later did I learn that one of our highly gifted laity, whom we had placed into leadership, had destroyed three other ministries through attempted leadership coups. She was now trying to take over a fourth.

When the dust settled, our baby church had dwindled to half its earlier attendance and was no longer growing. Those who remained were hurt and confused, with no emotional or spiritual energy to continue building. For the next three years, I did my best to shepherd the congregation, but God had not created me to be a pastoral-care pastor. No matter how hard I tried or how much I prayed, I knew I was out of my element. Day after day my stress level increased, until I felt my spiritual and emotional well was dry. I had nothing left to give to the congregation. I had experienced the "thrill of victory and the agony of defeat."

However, in the midst of this apparent failure, God was preparing me for a journey that would re-introduce me to my other passion: technology. He began showing me that technology and ministry were not incongruent at all, and that He had a plan and purpose to merge them in my life.

One day I received a phone call from the president of a Christian technology company. He was looking for a person who understood ministry, technology and marketing to spearhead a products division that would create software solutions for the ministry market. A month later I became director of product development and marketing, and I soon discovered that I loved my role. While I missed the spiritual formation aspects of ministry, I now worked closely with ministry leaders from around the United States, designing and developing software systems and solutions for ministry. One solution I am most proud of is Parent Pager (www.parentpager.com).

Yet, as the proverb goes, "All good things must come to an end." On September 11, 2001—with the fall of the Twin

Towers in New York—many technology companies like the one I served also fell into the dust. From this, God gave me a vision for my current ministry, E-Church Essentials (www.echurchessentials.com), and later its daughter division, AssessME.org (www.assessme.org).

E-Church Essentials took four years to conceive, design and develop. It also took every ounce of faith and finances that were available. Its purpose is to provide churches with an on-line platform to extend their Biblical mission mandates of evangelism, disciplemaking, Christ-centered community, equipping people for works of service, and mobilizing ministry teams.

AssessME.org is the premier on-line assessment center, designed exclusively for lay ministry mobilization and team building within the context of the local church. It enables church leaders to identify and position the right person with the right gifts, skills and temperament for any ministry position.

Every facet and passion of my life is fulfilled through E-Church Essentials and AssessME.org. I now know that I am accomplishing the mission for which I was created. It was no easy process getting to this point, however. I have often wished I had a mentor to come alongside me and help discern from the beginning what God envisioned and ordained for my life. Can you relate?

With an approach that is exceedingly practical, *Made for a Mission* is intended to be such a mentor. Like any good mentor, it may force you to address issues and questions in your life that you do not wish to uncover. Yet if you hope to honor Christ by completing your mission in this world, you must not let anything stand in your way. If your mission is from God, then all that is of God will support you in its completion, while all that is not of God will resist you fiercely.

One of my favorite movie series is the *Lord of the Rings* trilogy. This drama powerfully depicts the warfare between good and evil, and the mission that mere men are called to play in this epic struggle. Recently I watched one of these movies as I was recovering from a medical procedure and found myself identifying passionately with the challenges faced by Frodo, the primary character of the movie.

Frodo is a hobbit, a small human-like creature. Though by nature peace-loving and mild-mannered, Frodo is assigned the responsibility to save his world from evil. At times Frodo despairs over the weight of his mission; it feels overwhelming. Evil is doing all that it can to stop Frodo and conquer the world of Middle-Earth. At times the mission looks sure to fail, but in the end, good intervenes and evil is defeated.

Christ calls you and me to the same kind of epic struggle. In Matthew 28:19–20 we find His Great Commission, or what I prefer to call "Co-Mission," since He promises to accomplish the mission with us and through us: "Therefore go and make disciples of all nations, baptizing them in the name of the Father and of the Son and of the Holy Spirit, and teaching them to obey everything I have commanded you. And surely I am with you always, to the very end of the age."

Jesus gave the Great Co-Mission to a small crowd, yet His mandate applies to all people who choose to follow Him. Every Christ-follower is part of a common mission; yet how each person supports that mission is very different. The role you play will be unique, even as you are a unique creation. God did not give you a personalized mission strategy within the pages of the Bible. His mission strategy for you has been written within your DNA. You will better understand God's intended strategy for your life as you learn more about your created nature and allow the Holy Spirit to instruct and guide you. Throughout this discovery process, keep in mind that who you are, and how you should serve your Lord, should be affirmed by, and will never contradict, the Bible.

But I warn you: Don't expect your mission to be easy. Nor should you expect to complete your mission without placing significant reliance upon the Holy Spirit for guidance and support. "Easy faith" and "simple missions" are both oxymorons. The process of completing your mission will likely demand much; but as the saying goes, "The greater the risks, the greater the rewards."

"Easy faith" and "simple missions" are both oxymorons.

The Objectives

My first objective in writing this book is to help you identify and value the dynamics of your personal make-up, understanding that you have a unique design that is ideal for the mission God has called you to achieve.

My second objective is to coach you through a process of developing a Christ-centered life mission plan. This will include a personalized mission statement and a definition of appropriate ministry roles, as well as leadership team positions and team-support functions for which you are best suited. You will be guided through an analysys of how God has worked in your life and how He may wish to use you in the future. In addition, you will have an opportunity to assess your personal spiritual formation progress and identify developmental steps that will be beneficial in preparing you spiritually, emotionally and mentally for the task God has set before you.

My third objective is to instruct church leaders how to better mobilize people into personal ministry. In general, God calls you to serve Him as part of "Christ's body." For this reason *Made for a Mission* will address your personal ministry mission within the context of the local church or ministry organization. However, understanding how God created you to serve Him will be fruitless if your ministry organization is structured in a way that impedes you from serving effectively. We will evaluate organizational personalities and structures for the purpose of maximizing your church's ministry mobilization potential.

Note: Throughout the course of this book, you will be encouraged to take various assessments to help you better identify your unique design for ministry. Some assessments are included in this book. However many important assessments can only be accessed online from the AssessME.org website.

If your church or ministry organization has already created a ministry account with AssessME.org, you are encouraged to sign up within their account. This allows your leadership to view your results and support you in discovering your ministry fit. Please consult your ministry leadership regarding how to access their online assessment center.

Chapter 1

Preparing for Your Mission

A ny noble mission requires preparation. A Marine will spend many months, sometimes years, in training before he is ever sent on a mission. A doctor will study for eight or more years before undertaking the mission of curing disease and saving lives. In one way or another, every role that is highly valued within our culture requires preparation. Should it surprise us that God has established periods of training and preparation for His people to equip them for the mission for which He has created them?

Like a Marine, you and I must prepare to enter into battle—one that is spiritual in nature. It has been raging ever since Satan and one-third of the angels were thrown from heaven:

> And there was war in heaven. Michael and his angels fought against the dragon, and the dragon and his angels fought

back. But he was not strong enough, and they lost their place in heaven. The great dragon was hurled down—that ancient serpent called the devil, or Satan, who leads the whole world astray. He was hurled to the earth and his angels with him. (Rev. 12:7–9)

Satan and his fallen angels brought that war to earth. In a very real sense, every human being is born into a battlefield, and we all carry scars from trying to navigate and survive this war-torn world. God did not create us, however, to be mere survivors of this battleground, but victors through Christ our Lord—warriors and rulers over all creation (Gen. 1:26).

It was mankind's desire to be "like God, knowing both good and evil" (Gen. 3:5) that led to his fateful decision to rebel against his Creator, and he relinquished his throne over the earth to the Evil One. Thousands of years later, when Jesus was tempted in the wilderness, Satan proudly proclaimed his authority over the kingdoms of the world, and promised to hand them over if Jesus would bow down and worship him (Matt. 4:8–9).

Jesus rebuked Satan over the issue of who alone was worthy of worship, but He did not rebuke Satan's claim to dominion over this world. Jesus knew that God the Father had a plan, encapsulated in Ephesians 1:9–10:

> And he made known to us the mystery of his will according to his good pleasure, which he purposed in Christ, to put into effect when the times have reached their fulfillment— to bring all things in heaven and on earth together under one head, even Christ.

The Apostle Paul continues to tell us that all Christ-followers—those who believe that Jesus Christ is the Son of God and that He died as a payment for their sin—are chosen by God to help accomplish God's redemptive plan. We are no longer victims of the battlefield; we have been transformed into spiritual warriors. God calls us to enter into the fray of this fallen, battle-torn world, though our weapons are very different than those of the world.

> For though we live in the world, we do not wage war as the world does. The weapons we fight with are not the weapons of the world. On the contrary, they have divine power to demolish strongholds. We demolish arguments and every pretension that *sets itself up against the knowledge of God*, and we *take captive every thought* to make it obedient to Christ. And we will be ready to punish every act of disobedience, *once your obedience is complete.* (2 Cor. 10:3–6)

According to this passage, every Christ-follower must prepare for battle in three ways:

1. As the Holy Spirit leads, we remove everything from our lives that would keep us from knowing our God (we nurture our *relationship* with God).

2. We "take captive every thought" by submitting it to God (we transform our inner *thought life*).

3. In the righteousness we have in Christ, we demonstrate our love for God through our obedience to His commands (we master our *behaviors*).

My Relationship with God

My Spiritual Formation

My Thought-Life

My Behavioral-Life

This three-part preparation is a universal calling for every Christ-follower. It is your spiritual boot-camp, your basic training, which will continue for the rest of your life. Unless you take it seriously, you will not be properly prepared to accomplish God's ordained mission for your life.

Do You Choose to Accept the Mission?

In every episode of *Mission Impossible*, the self-destructing tape-recorded message always concluded with: "If you choose to accept this mission . . ." It is up to you to choose to pursue God's three-part preparation plan in your life. God will not force you to love Him or serve Him. He will not transform your inner thought-life or behaviors unless you let Him do it.

Fighting this battle requires total commitment. The Holy

Spirit will not allow you to be a double agent, seeking to serve the causes of two opposing forces. You will be challenged to pick one side or the other. There comes a point of decision in life when you must determine to either serve Christ or serve self—and in choosing to serve self, you choose to serve the Evil One.

> The Holy Spirit will not allow us to be double agents, seeking to serve the causes of two opposing forces.

Joshua presented this same challenge to the people of Israel:

> But if serving the LORD seems undesirable to you, then choose for yourselves this day whom you will serve, whether the gods your forefathers served beyond the River, or the gods of the Amorites, in whose land you are living. But as for me and my household, we will serve the LORD. (Joshua 24:15)

This is the day of decision. If you desire to realize your divinely created mission, you must have the determination and commitment of Joshua. You will soon discover that your commitment to follow Christ impacts every aspect of your being: your heart, your soul, your mind and your strength.

Identifying Your Felt Needs

Another term for the three-part preparation is *spiritual formation*, and it involves every aspect of your being—spiritual, mental, emotional and physical. This lifelong process renews your mind (Rom. 12:2) so you can know and act upon God's will; it re-forms your character so that your very nature increasingly exemplifies the character of Christ (Gal.

5:22–23); and it builds your love-relationship with your Lord, strengthening your faith and trust in His divine character and purposes.

As we noted before, the "Great Co-Mission" calls us to partner with Christ to make disciples of all nations. But what is our motivation for participating in this mission? Is it merely a sense of duty? The Bible makes it very clear that *love for God* should be our motivation. In fact God desires that we love Him above all else. When asked what the greatest commandment was, Jesus responded, "Love the Lord your God with all your *heart* and with all your *soul* and with all your *mind* and with all your *strength*" (Mark 12:30). The spiritual formation process attunes our entire being—heart, mind, spirit and body—toward Christ.

Because time and circumstances will test and refine our love and obedience to Christ, it is helpful for Christ-followers to continually evaluate their level of spiritual formation. This self-evaluation generally begins by exploring the maturity of our love-relationship with Christ as it impacts our heart, soul, mind and strength. The Biblical author, under the inspiration of the Holy Spirit, selected specific Greek words for heart, soul, mind and strength to signify that our entire being is to love the Lord. Let's explore these terms:

Heart—The Emotional Self

Have you ever considered that we are called to love the Lord our God with all of our emotions? We think of our "heart" as the seat of our emotions: we *feel*, *perceive* and *sense* with our hearts. When an important relationship ends, we use the phrase "brokenhearted" to illustrate the emotional pain we have experienced. For many people molded by our narcissistic culture, how they "feel" determines their sense of reality. For instance, they may divorce a spouse because they no longer "feel" in love.

Similarly, we may "feel" close to God or far away from Him, but our feelings, while valid, are a poor measure of reality. Although God promises us that He will never leave us (Heb. 13:5), we may at times feel distant from Him. Should we allow our feelings or God's promise to define reality? One of the most powerful tricks Satan uses to keep people immobilized for Christ is to damage their emotional well-being.

It is sad when people point to a church, a pastor or a Christ-follower as having deeply hurt them and then use those scars as excuses to refrain from attending church or serving Christ. While the pain may be real, we cannot allow it to keep us from following Christ and obeying His command to forgive those who sin against us (Matt. 6:12). We also must not let the pain keep us from Christ's call to serve Him in ministry. Spiritual formation of our heart requires that we surrender our feelings to the reality of God's promises and commandments.

You will soon have an opportunity to take a spiritual formation assessment. If you find that your heart is wounded, you are strongly urged to take appropriate steps to receive healing and to extend forgiveness. Your mission will require your heart to be healthy.

Soul—The Relational/Spiritual Self

We are also called to love the Lord with all of our soul—

the relational/spiritual self. Our souls long for connectedness with our Creator. We were designed to "walk with God in the garden" (Gen. 3:8), but like Adam and Eve, we often find ourselves ashamed of our sin and hiding in the bushes. We cover ourselves with fig leaves, telling everyone we are fine when inside we are lonely, weak and fallen. However, in Christ we can have a restored relationship with our Creator with no relational barriers between us. God gave us a powerful illustration of this truth at the moment of Christ's death upon the cross: "And when Jesus had cried out again in a loud voice, he gave up his spirit. At that moment the curtain of the temple was torn in two from top to bottom" (Matt. 27:50–51).

This passage refers to the curtain that hid the Most Holy Place of the temple, God's throne room, from being accessed by the common person due to the barrier of sin. When Christ died upon the cross, God placed my sin and your sin upon Jesus. He paid the death penalty for our sin. God split that curtain to send us a strong message, that no longer did a barrier exist between God and His creation. The author of Hebrews expands upon this important illustration:

> Therefore, brothers, since we have confidence to enter the Most Holy Place by the blood of Jesus, by a new and living way opened for us through the curtain, that is, his body, and since we have a great priest over the house of God, let us draw near to God with a sincere heart in full assurance of faith, having our hearts sprinkled to cleanse us from a guilty conscience and having our bodies washed with pure water. (Heb. 10:19–22)

Whatever may be keeping you from true relational intimacy with your Creator has already been addressed through the gift of Jesus Christ. Satan, however, knows that if he can keep you feeling guilty and fallen, you will feel inadequate to walk with God in the garden, let alone risk accomplishing the mission for which God created you. Rarely do soldiers who already feel defeated, and who hold little love for their leaders, ever risk much in a war; they are always quick to surrender. In contrast the Apostle Paul tells us that "in all things we are more than conquerors through him who loved us" (Rom. 8:37).

It is God's incredible love for you that draws you to Him and encourages you to live in relationship with Him. Your relationship with God is not about how many minutes you spend in devotions, or how long you pray, or the good works you do each day. God simply wants to walk and talk with you continually in the garden of your life. Your garden may be a battlefield full of weeds, but through the gift of Jesus Christ, the Master Gardener can root out the weeds that are choking your spiritual life and mission.

As you take the spiritual formation assessment, if you find that your soul has been damaged, and your relationship with God is not based upon love and intimacy, I urge you to learn to love and worship the God that loves you with an incredible love. Your mission will require your soul to be in love with God. You are to relate to Him intimately moment by moment, as you allow the Lord to renew your soul.

Mind – The Intellectual Self

We are called to love the Lord with all our intellect. But for many of us, our thinking has been formed predominately by the philosophies and values of our culture and not by God's Spirit and Scripture. In fact, most of us are unaware of how corrupted our minds are by the things of this world— so much so that we can no longer truly discern truth from falsehood and right from wrong. Jesus clearly instructs us, "I am the way the truth and the life, no man comes to the Father but through me" (John 14:6). Recent polls suggest, however, that many seemingly committed Christians are no longer confident that Jesus is the only way to God.[1]

This prevailing deception attacks the very foundation of the Great Co-Mission. Why should we strive to go throughout the whole world making disciples of Christ if there are other paths to God? Moral relativism, religious pluralism and a love for the things of this world are satanic attacks upon Christ's church, intended to influence us to be spiritually and missionally impotent.

As a student at a well-known Christian college, I saw one example of a church leader who failed to uphold scriptural truth and fell for the pluralistic philosophies of this world. On the first day of class, one of my professors told us that we would not only be studying the various religions to learn more about them; we would actually "practice" their worship, for that was the only way to truly relate to their religious culture. I immediately stood up in class and declared that the professor could fail me because the Bible clearly tells us not to worship other gods (Exod. 20:3). Numerous other students joined with me, and the professor was forced to back off from this inappropriate requirement. When church leaders no longer stand firm on the foundation of Scripture, how can we expect the average Christ-follower not to be deceived also?

A conscientious Christ-follower will test everything by the Word of God. Therefore we must know the Word of God well enough to "test" successfully. In Acts 17:11 the Bereans, are described "of more noble character than the Thessalonians, for they received the [gospel] message with great eagerness and examined the Scriptures every day to see if what Paul said was true." Loving the Lord with your intellect involves consistently testing, by the Word of God, the philosophies and messages that assault your mind every day. Remember, Satan's primary purpose for perpetuating religious pluralism and moral relativism is to diminish the passion and focus of your mission.

The Apostle Paul counseled his protégé Timothy:

> A time will come when men will not put up with sound doctrine. Instead, to suit their own desires, they will gather around them a great number of teachers to say what their itching ears want to hear. They will turn their ears from the truth and turn aside to myths. But you, keep your head in all situations, endure hardship, do the work of an evangelist, discharge all the duties of your ministry. (2 Tim. 4:3–5)

The time that is spoken of by Paul includes our time. Polls show us that even while we live in the "Communication Age," Biblical literacy is in serious decline. Relativism and pluralism are at an all-time high.[2]

The Bible is God's strategy handbook. When Christ-followers have a poor knowledge of Scripture, they fail to accomplish their ordained mission because they can't use the one and only spiritual offensive weapon God has given them (Eph. 6:17). Without the Sword of the Spirit, which is God's

Word, we literally become disarmed.

In John 17:17–18 Jesus prays for his disciples' mission in this world: "Sanctify them by the truth; your word is truth. As you sent me into the world, I have sent them into the world." To "sanctify" means to "cleanse of all impurities and to set apart for a special purpose." You have been called by God to be sanctified—cleansed and set apart for a special purpose—but it can only happen through the "washing of the Word." Paul tells us in Romans 12:2, "Do not conform any longer to the pattern of this world, but be transformed by the renewing of your mind. Then you will be able to test and approve what God's will is—his good, pleasing and perfect will."

When you take the spiritual formation assessment, if you find that your mind needs renewal by the Holy Spirit, I urge you to allow God to give you a new mind so that His thoughts become your thoughts, and His ways your ways. Your mission will require your mind to think rightly so that you may properly use the only offensive spiritual weapon at your disposal: the Word of God (Eph. 6:17).

> Our ministry service is a vital expression of our love for God and is not merely an "add-on" to our already busy lives. It should be at the core of our nature, impacting our family, career, schedule, and finances—literally every aspect of our lives.

Strength—The Actualized Self

God calls us to love Him with all our strength. Every action in our lives should be an expression of our faith and love of Christ. When we consider our life mission, this principle suggests that our priorities and decisions regarding everything we do should be re-aligned to make ministry our primary objective. Our ministry is a vital expression of our love for God and is not merely an "add-on" to our already busy lives. It should be at the core of our nature, impacting our family, career, schedule and finances—literally every aspect of our lives.

Yet while love is our motivation for ministry, our day-to-day ministry service will be sustained through the faith that God develops within us. It is impossible to separate our ministry actions from our faith in Christ. James tells us:

> What good is it, my brothers, if a man claims to have faith but has no deeds? Can such faith save him? Suppose a brother of sister is without clothes and daily food. If one of you says to him, "Go, I wish you well; keep warm and well fed," but does nothing about his physical needs, what good is it? In the same way, faith by itself, if not accompanied by action, is dead. But someone will say, "You have faith; I have deeds." Show me your faith without deeds and I will show you my faith by what I do" (James 2:14–18).

The Apostle Paul emphatically summarizes this point when he states that the only thing that matters in the Christian life is faith expressing itself through love (Gal. 5:6). All too often today people tend to compartmentalize their faith from their actions, treating their faith like a game of "Trivial Pursuit." Many people feel that to know some things *about* God is sufficient. However, the Bible does not validate a faith that exists apart from mission-action. We were made for a mission! Life in Christ is a call and commitment to action!

As we begin to invest ourselves in our God-ordained mission, we discover that it is greater than our abilities alone can achieve. We need God's help to complete His mission. When we are forced to rely on the work of God's Spirit in the midst of our mission, we see God "show up" and move in incredible ways, which in turn matures our faith. I believe God typically, but not exclusively, "shows up" and works miraculously when two conditions are present:

1. We must be willing to risk "self" in our mission—to risk failure.

2. We must come to the end of "self" as we seek to accomplish our mission—to admit that we are indeed failing and inadequate apart from his gracious intervention.

When these two conditions exist, God alone is able to receive the praise and glory as He intervenes to help us accomplish our mission objectives.

When I finished college, I believed God was calling me to continue my education in seminary— which did not thrill me in the least. It was in opposition to everything "I" wanted for "my" life. Yet every night as I had my devotional time with God, I had an overwhelming sense that I needed to go to seminary.

I resisted God's leading for two main reasons: 1) I did not see myself as the typical pastor; I was too entrepreneurial, creative and task-focused; 2) I had fallen into sin in my earlier years and due to my shame, felt unworthy to enter full-time ministry.

For over a year, I privately wrestled with God but told no one of my struggle. Finally I told God that I was never going to pray about this matter again. He must confirm my calling, or drop the subject. I did not want to pursue a path of my own making.

I had temporarily moved back into my parent's home that summer while I tried to decide whether to enter law school, go to seminary or pursue a teaching position. One night, two weeks after my ultimatum prayer, I returned home late from a date and discovered that my father was still awake watching television. He turned the television off, and we began to talk.

"So what are you going to do with your life?"

I told him I thought I would go to law school.

"Are you sure?"

"I don't understand it, but for the past two weeks I have felt impressed of the Lord that you are supposed to enter the ministry."

Remember, I had never told my father of my struggle. He had no idea that I had privately wrestled with God regarding my call to ministry for over a year. This was clearly the confirmation I was seeking.

God continued to confirm His leading in many other ways. I felt Him leading me to Trinity Evangelical Divinity School, but I had no money to pay for seminary. I didn't feel I could ask my church for support because Trinity wasn't associated with my denomination.

At that time I had started a singles ministry in my church. It had begun with a core of four singles, but, by the end of the year the group had grown to over 125 people. One day I received a phone call from the church secretary asking if I would be willing to meet with all the pastoral staff and the entire board. I was scared. What had I done?

When I arrived at the meeting, I was glad to be wearing my suit jacket—I was sweating profusely. But as the meeting began, the church leadership began to affirm me and the work I had done in establishing the singles ministry. They asked if I would consider going to seminary for pastoral training. I told them of my year-long struggle and how the call to ministry had recently been confirmed through my father; I also mentioned the school I believed God wanted me to attend. To my surprise they affirmed that Trinity was the ideal school for me and offered to support me with over $3,000 per year. I was off to seminary.

God supplied for me financially all through seminary, until the last quarter of my senior year. I was broke. Registration was only a few weeks away, and I needed $1,850 for tuition. I had only forty cents in my pocket! My first thought was to take out a student loan. On the way to the bank, however, I was suddenly overwhelmed with the thought that God might not want me to finish seminary. If so, I needed to submit to His leading. If He did want me to finish, then *He* needed to supply for me. After all, I didn't want to attend seminary in the first place!

Over the next few weeks, I was called to preach at two churches, and they each gave me a check for $100. A fellow student, who did not know of my need, gave me a check for $300 in an encouragement card. I now had $500 but was still $1,350 shy of the goal.

On the Saturday prior to registration, I received a letter from an elderly lady at a church where I had preached some months earlier. The letter read:

Dear David,

I was so blessed by your time with us, and now I feel God is leading me to bless you. When my husband died, he left me quite well off, so please do not worry about the gift.

Inside the envelope was a check for $1,500! God had not only supplied the money for my classes but also for my books—and I hadn't even thought about books!

There is an old saying among Christ-followers: *Where God guides, He provides.* Taking steps of faith and obedience in response to the leading of the Holy Spirit gives God the opportunity to manifest His presence and confirm that we are doing what He created us to do. And it is His confirmation that inspires us to love Him and trust Him all the more.

> Taking steps of faith and obedience . . . gives God the opportunity to manifest His support and confirmation that He is with us and that we are doing what He created us to do.

If the following spiritual formation assessment reveals that your faith has not been proven valid by your actions, will you not "risk all" for the sake of the One who loves you with an incredible love? Your mission requires you to trust God and walk by faith. In turn, God will enable you to accomplish the mission He has ordained for you.

The Spiritual Formation Assessment

The spiritual formation assessment process is designed to reveal your are spiritual strengths and weaknesses and to provide you with direction in pursuing spiritual maturity.

Remember that your spiritual formation process is your life-long bootcamp. God desires to prepare and equip you for the divine mission for which He created you.

Feel free to write in this book since it is designed to be a workbook. An online version of this assessment is available at www.assessme.org. If your church or ministry has already created an account with AssessME.org, you are encouraged to sign up with them and to consult your ministry leadership on how to access their online assessment center.

Special Note to Church Leaders: The online version of this assessment may be customized for use by your ministry.

Overview

The Spiritual Formation Assessment© has two parts: (It would be helpful to retake the assessment every six months to gauge your development.)

Part one identifies your current "felt need." A felt need is an individual's personal awareness of a need that may be so pervasive that it dominates all other developmental opportunities. For example: A recently divorced person may have a felt need for inner healing and restoration. Until that occurs, working on other areas of his or her life may be very difficult.

Part two identifies the specific spiritual formation areas in which you are *Breaking Ground, Taking Root* or *Reproducing Fruit.* Your scores within this portion of the assessment are related to, but not necessarily dependent upon, how long you have been a Christ-follower. For example, if you have been a Christ-follower for only six months and are having difficulty developing a prayer life, this struggle would appropriately fall into the *Breaking Ground* stage of spiritual development. However, if you have been a Christ-follower for six years and have the same score, then this would suggest a spiritual stagnation problem.

Part 1: Identify Your Current Felt Need

Jesus tells us that the greatest commandment is to "Love the Lord your God with all your *heart* and with all your *soul* and with all your *mind* and with all your *strength*," and that the second greatest commandment is to "Love your neighbor as yourself. There is no commandment greater than these" (Mark 12:29-31).

Instructions

1. In the Table on the next page, use the Order column to rank the statements from 1-4, ranging from your greatest perceived need (1) to your least perceived need (4).
2. In the Alpha Code line, enter the Alpha Code letters in the order that you identified.
3. In Appendix A – Felt-Need Reports, use your Alpha Code to identify your felt-need Profile. Enter your Profile in the blank on the next page.
4. As you read your felt-need Profile report, identify up to three strengths and three current issues that you affirm require immediate attention. Record these in the lines on the next page.

I Relate To God Through—	Prioritize These Statements:	Alpha Code	Order
HEART/emotions	I feel my most immediate need is to be emotionally restored.	A	
SOUL/spirit	I feel my most immediate need is to develop greater intimacy and trust in God	B	
MIND/intellect	I feel my most immediate need is to better understand God's Word so that I can apply it in my life.	C	
STRENGTH/ life-action	I feel my most immediate need is to live out my faith consistently through my words, actions and personal ministry.	D	

Alpha Code: _____

1   2   3   4

Profile: _____

(from Appendix A – Felt Needs Report)

My current strengths according to my report:

1. _____

_____

2. _____

_____

3. _____

_____

My current issues that require immediate attention according to my report:

1. _____

_____

2. _____
   _____
3. _____
   _____

Part 2: Spiritual Formation Progress Report

Part 2 of the Spiritual Formation Assessment presents five spiritual formation categories containing seven questions each.

Assessment Instructions:

1. In the blank below enter the date or life-stage during which you made a decision to follow Christ. Interpret your results according to how long you have been a Christ-follower.
2. In the Scores column of the assessment on the next page, rank each question on a scale of 1–5 where (1 = Not True and 5 = Very True).
3. In the Score Totals section, record the Sub-Total of the scores for each Category.

I have been a Christ-follower since _____.

Scores

1 = Not True | 2 = Somewhat True | 3 = Generally True |
4 = Typically True | 5 = Very True

Table 1-2

SCORES	Category 1: Believing in Christ
1 2 3 4 5	I agree with God that I have sinned and that the penalty for sin is death. I believe Jesus is God's Son, that He came to earth and died upon the cross to pay the pumishment due me for my sin, and that He rose again from the dead. I have placed my trust in Jesus Christ as my Savior from sin and as the Lord of my life.
1 2 3 4 5	I have been baptized in obedience to Jesus' command as a public expression of my faith in Him.
1 2 3 4 5	I believe the Bible is the inspired Word of God, is fully true and is the only infallible expression of truth about God and His will for my life.
1 2 3 4 5	I know without a doubt that if I died I would go to heaven, because of what Christ has done for me. I believe there is no way to God but through Jesus, who is the Way, the Truth and the Life.
1 2 3 4 5	I entrust my life and ministry daily to the empowerment of the Holy Spirit. This has resulted in a release of spiritual gifts within my life and a greater effectiveness in sharing my faith in Christ with others.
1 2 3 4 5	I look to God as the source of provision and protection for all my life, including finances, relationships, emotional health, ministry and guidance. I cast my cares on Him, walk in His peace and joy, and can tell specific stories about how God has been my provider, strength and guide.
1 2 3 4 5	I have read the entire Bible and understand and affirm the key doctrines of the Scriptures (For instance, I understand and affirm the Biblical doctrines regarding the nature of God, the Trinity, the kingdom of God, the covenants with Abraham and Moses, the new covenant in Christ, the Atonement, salvation by grace through faith alone, sanctification, baptism, the Lord's Supper, what it means to be "in Christ," the empowerment of the Holy Spirit, the second coming of Christ and the authority of Christ).

SCORES	Category 2: Belonging in Christ's Body
1 2 3 4 5	I attend church services almost every week and participate in the community life of my church.
1 2 3 4 5	I understand why community life is vital for Christian living, and so I participate within a small group and/or am connected in relationships with other Christ-followers who provide encouragement and accountability.
1 2 3 4 5	I consistently seek to be authentic and to love, accept and forgive people in my family, church and community.
1 2 3 4 5	I affirm that if I am to serve Christ effectively, the Bible calls me to love, support and nurture others inside and outside the fellowship of believers, and to honor and respect those whom God has placed in authority over me—especially leaders who faithfully teach the Bible.
1 2 3 4 5	Because the Bible calls me to live in fellowship with other Christ-followers, it is important that I commit myself to a local body of believers; and personally participate in the mission to which Christ has called them.
1 2 3 4 5	I believe God has given me gifts, talents and finances with the expectation that I would use them to extend His kingdom in this world, and to strengthen the spiritual health and ministry of my local church.
1 2 3 4 5	I understand the meaning and purpose of tithing, and I give 10% of my income (possibly more) to God.

SCORES	Category 3: Being with God
1 2 3 4 5	I have meaningful times with God each day, including time in God's Word, prayer, praise and listening to God's voice.
1 2 3 4 5	I know how to recognize God's voice as He speaks to me during times when I listen in silence or while pondering His written Word. When I hear His voice, I consistently obey His direction.

1 2 3 4 5	I feel free and uninhibited in my worship of God, both in my heart and through my outward expression. As I worship, my thoughts are captivated by God's love and holiness, and I feel His presence stirring deep within me.
1 2 3 4 5	I am confident of my heavenly Father's unconditional, boundless love and acceptance, and I know He has a good plan for my life.
1 2 3 4 5	I am overwhelmed by the holiness of God and walk daily in the fear (reverential awe) of the Lord.
1 2 3 4 5	I spend significant time each day in meaningful prayer, and as I pray, I have a deep confidence that God hears me and will answer my prayers.
1 2 3 4 5	I have learned to give thanks in all circumstances and no longer grumble or complain. Because I know that God is at work, I have a positive outlook on my life and future. I am deeply thankful for my spouse (if married), my family, my friends, my church and the many blessings God has given me.

SCORES   Category 4: Being Transformed

1 2 3 4 5	I believe that I am accountable to God and that He is the "Lover of my soul" who will direct and discipline me for my good and lead me into His righteousness. I also value the assistance of healthy and godly accountability relationships that enrich my life with wisdom, support and encouragement so that I may grow strong in my faith.
1 2 3 4 5	While I still occasionally sin, I am free and am no longer a slave to sinful behaviors and addictions that once held me captive.
1 2 3 4 5	I know the Holy Spirit is at work in my life because I and others recognize that I am growing in love, joy, peace, patience, kindness, goodness, faithfulness, gentleness and self-control.
1 2 3 4 5	Those who know me well would say that I live in healthy, loving and honoring relationships with others (family, friends and co-workers) and that I observe godly and appropriate sexual boundaries.

1 2 3 4 5	In my closest relationships (with spouse, children, parents and friends) I listen to them effectively, I seek to understand and attend to their needs, and I am able to resolve differences. I have fulfilling relationships that meet mutual needs and expectations.
1 2 3 4 5	My finances (or if married, "our finances") are in Biblical order. I know that God owns all that I have and I seek to spend His money in accordance with His guidance and Biblical principles. I am a diligent worker. I am decreasing or have eliminated my debt. I am saving and giving faithfully to my local church and other Kingdom causes.
1 2 3 4 5	I understand and affirm Biblical moral and ethical principles, and am committed to living out the positions expressed in God's Word, even when these are socially or culturally unpopular. (For instance, I know and live according to the Biblical standards concerning sexual purity, substance abuse, marriage and remarriage, finances, honesty, abortion, racial reconciliation, care for the poor, the widow and the orphan, honor and obedience to authority, and social justice.)

SCORES	Category 5: Bringing Christ to Others

1 2 3 4 5	I know how to share the Good News of Jesus with others. I feel Jesus' love and compassion for those who do not have salvation in Him and actively pursue relationships with them in order to share the love and Good News of Christ.
1 2 3 4 5	I actively participate in outreach and evangelistic opportunities offered by my church.
1 2 3 4 5	I know the gifts the Holy Spirit has given to me. I have been equipped by my leaders to consistently use my gifts to love, serve and encourage others in their faith.
1 2 3 4 5	I have been equipped to effectively minister to others through prayer and the Word of God. I regularly minister in prayer to others and seek to share Biblical insights God gives me to build others up in their faith.

1 2 3 4 5	I am investing myself in the personal and spiritual life of at least one other person outside my immediate family. This "investment" has resulted in spiritual "dividends" in my life and in the life of those God has called me to serve.
1 2 3 4 5	I am actively serving as a spiritual mentor, and I understand how to guide others in their spiritual journey.
1 2 3 4 5	I have been tested over time by my spiritual leaders and have been found to be faithful to Christ and to God's Word. For this reason I have been asked to serve as a leader in our local congregation (for example: a small group leader, teacher, pastor, evangelist, ministry director or ministry coordinator).
Score Totals	1) Believing in Christ Sub-Total: _____ 2) Belonging in Christ's Body Sub-Total: _____ 3) Being with God Sub-Total: _____ 4) Being Transformed Sub-Total: _____ 5) Bringing Christ to Others Sub-Total: _____

Report Instructions: Plot your spiritual formation scores on the Table on the following page.

1. Plot each category score by placing a dot along the axis associated with the appropriate spiritual formation category.

2. Draw a line connecting the five dots to create your trend-report. Use a specific color ink/pencil for your trend report and date it so that when you re-take the assessment every six months or so (using a different color of ink or pencil each time) you will be able to view graphically your developing spiritual maturity.

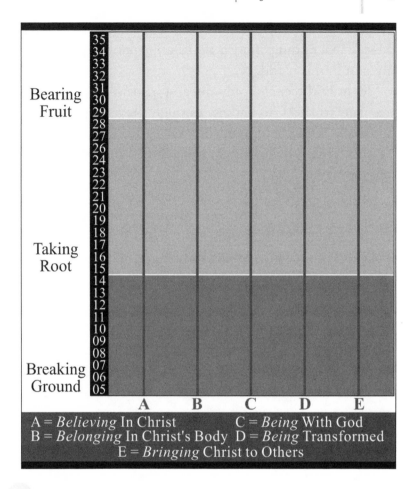

	A	B	C	D	E
Bearing Fruit	35 34 33 32 31 30 29				
Taking Root	28 27 26 24 23 22 21 20 19 18 17 16 15				
Breaking Ground	14 13 12 11 10 09 08 07 06 05				

A = *Believing* In Christ   C = *Being* With God
B = *Belonging* In Christ's Body   D = *Being* Transformed
E = *Bringing* Christ to Others

Assessment Conclusion

By analyzing your individual scores and taking into consideration your felt-need priorities, it is possible to construct a fairly clear picture of your present spiritual formation progress. Reflect upon your report summary, possibly discuss it with your pastor or small group leader, and spend time in prayer to determine your next step toward maturity. While God can and does use us in spite of our failings and immaturity, there will likely be some areas you need to address so that nothing hinders the fulfillment of your ordained mission in this world.

Identify three, and only three, spiritual formation areas that you will seek to address through prayer, by the Holy Spirit and with the support of your pastor or small group. The objective is to identify spiritual formation goals for each developmental area.

In six months retake this assessment to guage your progress, and repeat these steps by identifying and addressing three new spiritual formation goals. You may wish to make this process an ongoing spiritual formation discipline.

Spiritual Formation Goals

1. _____
   _____
   _____

2. _____
   _____
   _____

3. _____
   _____
   _____

Spiritual Maturity

The Apostle Paul holds himself up as an example of spiritual maturity. We find his passion for mission exploding in the words of Philippians 3:7–16:

But whatever was to my profit I now consider loss for the sake of Christ. What is more, I consider everything a loss compared to the surpassing greatness of knowing Christ Jesus my Lord, for whose sake I have lost all things. I consider them rubbish, that I may gain Christ and be found in him, not having a righteousness of my own that comes from the law, but that which is through faith in Christ—the righteousness that comes from God and is by faith. I want to know Christ and the power of his resurrection and the fellowship of sharing in his sufferings, becoming like him in his death, and so, somehow, to attain to the resurrection from the dead. Not that I have already obtained all this, or have already been made perfect, but I press on to take hold of that for which Christ Jesus took hold of me. Brothers, I do not consider myself yet to have taken hold of it. But one thing I do: Forgetting what is behind and straining toward what is ahead, I press on toward the goal to win the prize for which God has called me heavenward in Christ Jesus. *All of us who are mature should take such a view of things.* And if on some point you think differently, that too God will make clear to you. Only let us live up to what we have already attained.

Let's review Paul's mission priorities in a paraphrased summary form and make it personal using the pronoun "I":

- I no longer seek what benefits me but am willing to sacrifice my ambitions for the sake of Christ. I invest my time, energy and resources into knowing Christ and His power, rather than pursuing the things of this world.
- I realize that serving Christ, and sacrificing all that I have for Him, does not make me a righteous person.

- I am committed to identifying myself with Christ in such a manner that I personally experience both His power and His sufferings in my life.
- I am pressing forward to achieve the purpose for which God called and saved me, and to gain the prize that God has set before me—to hear Him say, "Well done, good and faithful servant."
- I am able to shed my past failures and feelings of inadequacy so that I can live for Christ unencumbered and be faithful to His calling each day.
- I consider myself mature in Christ and fully agree and identify with Paul's passion for mission.

Humbling isn't it? But remember that Paul started his spiritual journey on the Damascus Road asking, "Who are You, Lord?" He didn't even know who God was at that point. He would never have been able to make those statements at the beginning of his spiritual formation process. But Paul allowed the Holy Spirit to reshape him from the inside out so that he could become a worthy servant of Jesus Christ.

When we commit our lives to Christ, the Holy Spirit begins His work to transform, empower and call us into ministry service. The Spirit desires to bring us to the place where we are totally submissive to the will and purposes of our God.

Unfortunately many people today consider themselves to be Christians, yet they have not reached a point in their faith-walk in which they are ready to lay themselves, their desires, wants and ambitions upon the altar of Christ. To a certain extent this is true for every Christ-follower. We are the proverbial "living sacrifice" (Rom. 12:1) that keeps crawling off the altar whenever the flames get too hot. In time, however, as we continually submit to the will and purposes of Jesus Christ, we will find ourselves able to withstand the altar's flames. As we mature, we will find ourselves crawling off the altar less and glorifying Christ more each day.

Chapter 2

Form
Follows Function

Take a moment and look around you. Do you see a clock, a computer or a television? Every item you see was created for a particular function, and its form is best suited to accomplish that function. Designers refer to this principle as the item's "form factor." An item's form is determined by the function for which it was created.

The same is true about you. You have a unique "form factor"—your personality. The personality God has given you is not a mistake. He created you, and in His omniscience He knew the good works—the function—that He prepared in advance for you (Eph. 2:10). God in His grace will "equip you with everything good to do his will" (Heb. 13:21; see also 2 Cor. 9:8 and Phil. 1:6); this includes your personality.

Value Your Form Factor

We often tend to devalue or even resent the person God

has created us to be. We envy the personality traits and behavior in those we respect, and we want to be like them. Parents, teachers and others sometimes fuel this discontent with negative comments such as, "Why can't you be more like your sister or brother?"

I believe Satan is behind these self-destructive feelings. He stands condemned and defeated because of the work of Jesus Christ upon the cross, but like a vicious wounded animal, he still tries to do as much damage as possible before his end. If he can get us to doubt or devalue our God-ordained personality and innate worth as a child of God, he can immobilize us so that we fail to realize our incredible potential in Christ and fail to fulfill the mission for which we were created.

But God does not want you to be immobilized and weak. Ephesians 1:11–14 makes it abundantly clear that who you are is a significant part of God's purpose in this world:

> In him we were also *chosen*, having been *predestined according to the plan* of him who works out everything *in conformity with the purpose of his will*, in order that we, who were the first to hope in Christ, *might be for the praise of his glory*. And *you also were included in Christ* when you heard the word of truth, the gospel of your salvation. Having believed, you were *marked in him with a seal, the promised Holy Spirit*, who is *a deposit guaranteeing our inheritance* until the redemption of those who are God's possession—to the praise of his glory.

I have italicized several words and phrases in this passage so that we might explore them more fully and not merely gloss over them. They are essential to our sense of self-value in Christ.

D. *Chosen*—The Greek word denotes that you have been selected from among the billions of people that God has created throughout history to be in a relationship with Him and to serve Him according to His divine mission. You are not a random accident or the consequence of a haphazard evolutionary process. Acts 17:26 states, "From one man he made every nation of men, that they should inhabit the whole earth; *and he determined the times set for them and the exact places where they should live.*" Your existence at this unique time in history, and this unique geographical location, is by God's design.

In the Old Testament, Queen Esther was a Jewess in the court of Xerxes, king of Persia (Iran). Her uncle Mordecai learned of a plot among some Persian leaders to purge the land of all Jews (an early satanic attempt at a holocaust) and he appealed to Esther to use her influence as queen to help her people. Esther was deeply afraid, but Mordecai gave her this warning: "If you remain silent at this time, relief and deliverance for the Jews will arise from another place, but you and your father's family will perish. And who knows but that you have come to royal position for such a time as this" (Esther 4:14).

God had set the times for Esther and the exact place where she should live. In the same way He has positioned you "for such a time as this." If you remain silent, God's purposes will be accomplished "from another place," but you will miss the great honor of trusting and serving your God. God's divine purposes will be accomplished with or without you—it is your choice. God calls you to be set apart as a holy servant, designed and positioned by God for a very important mission.

(2) . *Predestined*—This word does not carry with it the secular connotation of "fate," as if we had no ability to choose; we are not the "playthings of the gods," as the ancient Greeks believed. Instead it implies that our omniscient Creator, knowing all things and seeing the future in infinite detail, foresaw this very moment in time and space and determined to create you, fashioning you to fit perfectly into His divine plan at this exact moment in history.

We can't properly understand this concept apart from the Biblical notion that God indeed does have a wonderful and glorious plan. For some reason we cannot begin to fathom, He wants you and me to participate in the unfolding of that plan. When we accept God's plan for us and the vital role we play in His universal mission, we join with Paul in asking, "If God is for us, who can be against us?" (Rom. 8:30).

(3) · *The Plan*—God's plan is in many ways a mystery, visible to us only in broad brushstrokes. To help us understand His plan, God has given us the Bible, His only authoritative written communication. It outlines His mission in this world: to destroy all that is evil and to reclaim, through the person and work of His Son, Jesus Christ, those who are willing to follow Him.

You and I were integrated into God's divine plan when we "heard the word of truth, the gospel" (Eph. 1:13). Why were we included? ". . . to be for the praise of his glory" (Eph. 1:14). Our sole reason for existence on this planet, as Christ-followers, is to bring glory to God. There is no higher calling. How we best bring glory to Him is not necessarily by doing good works, going to church or even tithing sacrificially. We bring glory to God when we discover and fulfill our predestined role in God's divine plan.

We were once like a jigsaw puzzle piece that was lost. Without that lost piece, the picture of God's plan of redemption was not complete. But now that we have been "found," it is time for us to "find our fit" and complete our portion of the puzzle.

> Our sole reason for existence on this planet, as Christ-followers, is to bring glory to God. There is no higher calling . . . . We bring glory to God when we discover and fulfill our predestined role in God's divine plan.

Marked with a Seal— Ephesians 1:13 tells us that every Christ-follower has a divine mark within—the mark of the Holy Spirit. The Spirit's mark is intended to be an obvious assurance of the reality of our eternal relationship with Christ. How do we recognize His mark? We find the answer in the four distinct phases of the Holy Spirit's working in our lives. Each phase of the Spirit's work encourages us to persevere to the next level of spiritual development. This four-phase process is outlined in Romans 8:28–31:

> And we know that in all things God works for the good of those who love him, who have been called according to his purpose. [Note the ultimate goal!] For those God foreknew he also *predestined* to be conformed to the likeness of his Son, that he might be the firstborn of many brothers. And those he *predestined*, he also *called*; those he *called*, he also *justified*; those he *justified*; he also *glorified*. What can we say in response to this? If God is for us, who can be against us?

The work of the Spirit is clearly a process, with the ultimate goal being our glorification. We can depict His work graphically as a series of steps. Unfortunately, many Christ-followers reach step #3, justification, and rest secure in their salvation. But our salvation is not the ultimate goal of the Spirit's work. The ultimate goal is our glorification!

Phase #4: Glorified
The Holy Spirit glorifies us as we accomplish His purpose.

Phase #3: Justified
The Holy Spirit justifies us —we are forgiven through Christ.

Phase #2: Called
The Holy Spirit calls us into a relationship with Christ.

Phase #1: Predestined
The Holy Spirit foreknew us before creation.

Remember, our highest calling is to bring glory to God. In this passage we are told that the Holy Spirit wants to bring glory to us. The reality is that our glory and God's glory are intimately intertwined. As we bring glory to God by serving Him according to our divinely inspired form factor, He in turn glorifies us!

Each step in our spiritual development is evidence that a real God is at work in our real lives. But it is in step #4, glorification, where life in the Spirit gets very interesting; here the Christ-follower begins to experience the guidance, gifting, empowerment and prayer of the Holy Spirit.

We should never make the mistake of thinking, as the Holy Spirit calls, justifies and glorifies us, that our experience will be the same as everyone else's experience. We are unique creations with unique personality traits. Taken as a whole, all personality types present a picture of God's nature. After all, we were all formed in His image (Gen. 1:26).

Though the Bible does not use the word "personality," the human body is presented as a visual aid to explain our unique differences:

> For we were all baptized by one Spirit into one body—whether Jews or Greeks, slave or free—and we were all given the one Spirit to drink. Now the body is not made up of one part but of many. If the foot should say, "Because I am not a hand, I do not belong to the body," it would not for that reason cease to be part of the body. And if the ear should say, "Because I am not an eye, I do not belong to the body," it would not for that reason cease to be part of the body. If the whole body were an eye, where would the hearing be? If the whole body were an ear, where would the sense of smell be? *But in fact God has arranged the parts of the body, every one of them, just as he wanted them to be.* If they were all one part, where would the body be? As it is, there are many parts but one body. (1 Cor. 12:13–20)

The Apostle Paul places this image of the many parts of the body in the middle of a discussion on *spiritual gifts*, and he refers specifically to other differences—*ethnicity* ("Jew or Greek") and *social position* ("slave or free"). So the concept certainly applies as well to differences in personality.

I once struggled with an issue of personality style: the feeling that I was not a "typical pastor." It was a profound revelation to me—and a great relief—when I finally realized that who I am was by God's intentional design and that my unique role within the ministry of Christ was vitally important. God had positioned me "just where he wanted me to be." God never wanted me to be "typical." In fact, "a-typical" probably meant that God had a special mission for me that only an "a-typical" pastor could fulfill!

For many years I had been an ear wishing to be an eye. I had devalued who God had made me to be, wishing instead to re-create myself in the image of my own choosing. As long as I tried to be something I was never intended to be, and do things I was never intended to do, I could not experience the "glorification" of the Holy Spirit. Instead I experienced stress, anxiety and failure.

Knowing and honoring our place within the body and service of Christ is fundamental to effective ministry. Everything we say and do, and the spiritual gifts we exercise, are all filtered through our personality. Since the era of Hippocrates, 2,400 years ago,[1] philosophers have studied personality traits and have tried to categorize the attributes that most influence our makeup. Because human beings are so complex, it is unrealistic to think that we could ever fully define any person. However we can identify traits common to people who possess similar personality characteristics. Today it is common to assess personalities based upon four quadrants of influence:

- Our Relationship Style
- Our Information Assimilation Style
- Our Decision-Making Style
- Our Environmental Style

The chart below gives an expanded explanation of how the four quadrants influence who we are and how we will most likely function as we seek to accomplish God's ordained mission for our lives.

The Four Defining Personality Quadrants

Relational Style

Independent < > Social

Your Relational Style determines how you relate to others, and whether you are energized by being with people, or need to be emotionally recharged by having time alone.

Information Assimilation Style

Abstract < > Concrete

Your Information Assimilation Style determines your information gathering preferences. An Abstract profile prefers concepts, ideas, theories, and philosophies. A Concrete profile prefers facts, tangible evidence, and proven methods.

Decision-Making Style

Head < > Heart

Your Decision-Making Style identifies whether your decisions are based more upon logic and facts (Head), or by perceptions and feelings (Heart).

Environmental Style

Systematic < > Adaptive

Your Environmental Style identifies how you relate to the world around you. Whether by trying to structure your world (Systematic), or are able to flex and flow with the demands of ever changing circumstances (Adaptive).

Some people shy away from personality assessments, believing that "if you really knew me, you wouldn't like me." It's certainly true that we are all fallen creatures; even the Apostle Paul called himself a "wretched man" (Rom. 7:24). Yet God knows us best, and He not only likes us, He loves us with an infinite love. A personality assessment doesn't display our depravity and failings to the world; it affirms our value and mission in this world. Without a solid appreciation of the personality God gave us, it is very likely that we will never truly understand the mission He created us to fulfill.

However, many people still fear personality assessments. In one of my early ministries, I wanted to better understand how to relate to and work with the elder board. I asked each one of the elders to take the DiSC® personality assessment. The head elder was very fearful and distrustful of such tools. Unknown to me, he determined to intentionally misrepresent himself in the assessment. When I received the reports, I openly reviewed them with each person on the board. In each case, the board members found the assessment to be very insightful and helpful—until we read the head elder's report.

Immediately, all the members of the board knew something was wrong. The report did not describe him. The elder then admitted that he had intentionally lied on his assessment to "prove" that personality assessments could not be trusted. In fact, all this elder proved was that it is wise to test the results of any assessment report against our experience and knowledge of the person. Those who are closest to us often know us better than we know ourselves. Ministry leaders who use assessment tools responsibly will verify the results through a personal interview with the ministry candidate.

We all have been designed by God for a unique purpose. It is crucial that we understand who God made us to be and that we appreciate and value our uniqueness. Understanding who we are gives us permission to say "no" to ministry opportunities that are an improper fit for us and allows us to focus upon ministry opportunities appropriate to our divine design.

Anyone who has been in ministry for any amount of time will be familiar with church members who have difficulty saying "no"—those who are driven and motivated by guilt or obligation. Serving for the sake of service is not necessarily a positive ministry attribute. We can become so busy doing "good things" that we fail to achieve the true mission for which God created us.

A reporter once asked Thomas Edison for the secret to his success. Edison replied, "We all have 24 hours in a day, and roughly the same number of years in our life. I choose to spend my time accomplishing one thing until it is complete. Others choose to spend their time doing many things." Our personality was given to us by God to facilitate our divinely ordained ministry purpose. The secret to our success will be to allow ourselves permission to focus upon that "one thing."

It should be clear by now that your personality has been given to you by God to support your unique ministry mission. For this reason we will predominantly use the term "ministry temperament" rather than personality for the remainder of this book.

To help you have a more complete understanding of this chapter, please take the assessment that follows.

ePersonality© Overview

The ePersonality© worksheet has two parts. *Part one* will help you to identify your ministry temperament based upon your unique personality dynamics. *Part two* allows you to validate the ePersonality© report, based on your life experiences, and to prayerfully assess how God desires to work through your personality for His purposes.

Part 1: Summarize Your ePersonality Profile

Instructions

1. Go to www.assessme.org to take your ePersonality© assessment online.
2. Print your ePersonality© report from the website or refer to your ePersonality© report in Appendix B. (Note: Appendix B includes all sixteen reports.)
3. Use the information from your ePersonality© report to complete the Personality Profile Worksheet.

Personality Profile Worksheet

A. My ministry temperament profile title: _____
   _____

B. My heart's cry statement (found immediately below the title): _____
   _____
   _____

C. My profile highlights:

1. _____
2. _____
3. _____
4. _____
5. _____

D. My bar graph scores reflect that I am dominant in the following areas:

How I Relate to People

• _____ **Independent.** I tend to require time alone to recharge after social situations. I can work well with people or by myself. I tend to be task or systems oriented when seeking to accomplish a goal.

• _____ **Relational.** I tend to require social interaction within my life. I find that I am energized by being with people and can be most productive when serving on a team or with a group. I may care more about how people are doing personally than whether a particular task or goal is accomplished.

How I Process Information

• _____ **Abstract.** I prefer to work with ideas, concepts, theories, theology and philosophy. I may be quite visionary and prefer to think in terms of "what could be" rather than being satisfied with "what is."

• _____ **Concrete.** I prefer hard facts and statistics. I care deeply about gathering practical information that can be practically applied. I tend to be distrustful of unproven theories or entrepreneurial vision.

How I Process Decisions

- _____ **Head.** I tend to make decisions based upon what seems logical and provable. I generally gather information and statistics prior to making a decision, and once a decision is made, I may appear inflexible unless more information can be presented which would alter my conclusions.

- _____ **Heart.** I tend to make decisions based upon how I feel would be right and best for the people the decision would impact. I care less about "facts" and more about the "consequences" of my decisions.

How I Relate to the World around Me

- _____ **Systematic.** I prefer order, rules and logical lists. I prefer to have a check-off list of duties to accomplish, and I gain satisfaction from checking items off my "to do" list. I am resistant to change unless the change is well planned and intentional.

- _____ **Adaptive.** I prefer to go-with-the-flow. I expect the unexpected and look forward to new experiences. I resist being "put in a box" and tend to view rules (or a plan) as a "guide" rather than as "law." I value and anticipate change.

E. I affirm within myself the following STRENGTHS as noted in my profile report:

1. _____

2. _____

3. _____

4. _____

5. _____

F.   I affirm within myself the following WEAKNESSES as noted in my profile report:

1.   _____

2.   _____

Part 2: Apply Your ePersonality© Profile

A.   Please reflect upon your life and note specific service (or work) situations in which you felt were "most fulfilling" or "most satisfying." Did those experiences align with your personality profile report? If so, how did your experiences align with your personality profile report?

_____

_____

_____

_____

_____

_____

_____

_____

B.   Describe service (or work) situations that caused significant stress within your life. Did those situations align with your personality profile, or did they demand that you serve in a manner that did not fit who God made you to be?

_____

_____

_____

_____

_____

_____

_____

C. Given what I have learned about my personality, if I am to honor who God made me to be, I should:

Seek ministry opportunities that require the following traits:

1. _____

2. _____

3. _____

4. _____

5. _____

Say "No" to ministry opportunities that require the following traits:

1. _____

2. _____

3. _____

4. _____

5. _____

D. Please summarize your personality in your own words: *God made me to be a person designed to . . .* _____

_____

_____

_____

_____

_____

Mission Myopia

Now that you have learned about your ministry temperament, you may be curious as to how your ministry temperament fits into the mission of your local church or ministry organization. Just as you have begun a process of self-discovery, your church leadership may also need to learn more about themselves and how their combined personalities define the personality of the ministry organization.

Every church organization exhibits a unique organizational personality. An organization's personality type enables its leadership to effectively recruit and mobilize people with certain ministry temperaments, while impeding the recruitment and mobilization of others who possess differing ministry temperaments.

Within Christ's universal church, every individual is a vital member with an essential ministry role. A local church, however, cannot be as inclusive of all types of people. Its own organizational personality traits enable it to mobilize certain ministry temperaments into service, while unfortunately impeding other ministry temperaments. Ministry mobilization difficulties are most often the direct result of institutional dynamics (*i.e.*, organizational personality dynamics) rather than the fault of the individual church member. Sadly, however, pastoral leaders often see the lack of ministry participation and blame their membership for being "uncommitted."

As I speak about team building and exhibit AssessMe.org at various ministry conferences around the country, I have observed a consistent pattern: Pastors of churches with fewer than 400 members are most likely to criticize their members for a lack of commitment. I constantly hear negative statements such as, "I can't get my people to do anything;" or "I can barely get my people to come to church regularly; I doubt I could get them to go online to take assessments."

Ironically, these frustrated pastors often have a highly *relational* ministry temperament. As such, they are very likable people but possess few skills at developing ministry structures or teams. When the church was smaller, these pastors found that they could effectively minister to others through personal visitations, lunch meetings and simple Sunday programming. However as the church began to grow, its organizational dynamics became far too complex for the pastor's relational ministry style. The relational pastor generally tries to "solve" the problem by making repeated appeals from the pulpit for "help"; yet because little organizational structure exists, the people simply do not know how to support their church or pastor.

I am convinced that these discouraged pastors are generally godly men who want to serve their Lord and their people faithfully. I am also convinced that their people likewise desire to serve their Lord and other people faithfully. I do not believe the ministry mobilization problem resides with the people or the pastor but with the organization's personality dynamics.

Organizational personalities are based upon the unique mix of dominant influencers within the organization. These influencers may or may not include church board members. These influencers may or may not even include the pastor(s). How do you discover the dominant influencers within any organization? Simply ask the members of the organization.

Effective pastors are not only aware of who the key influencers are within the organization; they are able to successfully navigate the various evolutions in organizational personality as the organization matures. Until the pastoral leadership is willing to discover and address the organizational personality issues that are impeding people from participating in ministry, the church will continue to limp along in survival-mode with the pastor doing most of the ministry and feeling isolated and abandoned by the membership.

> Our ministry temperament was designed to integrate with other minisry temperaments so that together, we can accomplish for Christ far more than we could ever accomplish individually.

Christ never desired His followers to minister in isolation. He always sent His disciples out in teams of two or more (Luke 10:1). Similarly, the apostles always had at least one or two support staff. Remember: We all need each other, and it is together that we best represent the God who created all of us in His image. Our ministry temperament was designed to integrate with other ministry temperaments so that together we can accomplish for Christ far more than we could ever accomplish individually.

Why do we need each other? Let me illustrate by using my own personal profile. I care deeply about people; however, God designed me to be a builder of ministry systems and structures that help others to care for and spiritually nurture the body of Christ. As a task-focused "systems man," I will never be able to exhibit the same warmth and compassion that comes so naturally to the relational pastors mentioned previously. In the same manner, people-oriented individuals will not excel at creating ministry systems and structures that facilitate broad-based ministry impact. In God's global mission to redeem the world, He has determined that all ministry temperaments should support one another to help accomplish His mission.

> Mission myopia exists whenever we consolidate around us people who possess a similar ministry temperament, or impose our ministry temperament upon those closest to us.

Mission Myopia

It may surprise you to learn that even though the Bible is abundantly clear about the many parts of Christ's body, when it comes to building ministry teams, many Christians and Christian leaders somehow forget that God created human diversity. It should be self-evident that not every Christ-follower will look, sound or act like every other Christ-follower.

However, the Church often suffers from what I call "mission myopia." The Oxford American Dictionary defines myopia as "nearsightedness" or "lack of imagination or intellectual insight." Mission myopia exists whenever we consolidate around ourselves people who possess a similar ministry temperament or impose our ministry temperament—and its way of perceiving and serving—upon those closest to us.

The problem of mission myopia was illustrated quite profoundly to me some time ago. I received a phone call from a pastor asking if I would be willing to meet with him. As we sat and talked, he began to unload his frustration with his church board. He felt they were lacking in integrity and failing to fulfill their ministry obligations, and that they might have to be removed from the church board.

Over my years of pastoral ministry and consulting with ministry leaders, I had come across some difficult and even unhealthy church boards; but, the prospect of removing an entire board seemed quite extreme. As we talked the situation became clear: This pastor had led his church leadership team through a strategic planning process that advocated and blessed only one ministry style—the pastor's. In theory, the board members had agreed that the method outlined by their pastor was very important for their church. In practice, however, it soon became clear that most of the board members were incapable of sustained personal ministry using the pastor's methodology.

I asked this pastor to describe specific personality traits for each board member. As he did so it became very clear to me that this well-meaning pastor was violating God's ordained mission for each one of his board members. This ministry board consisted of individuals who were strong visionary leaders and project administrators. They were task-oriented and systems-oriented people. In contrast, the pastor's personal style was relational, focusing on one-to-one or small group interpersonal ministry.

This pastor did not mean to sin against his board, but in fact, by trying to treat each board member as an "eye," to see and do things his way, he was violating each board member's divinely inspired ministry temperament. This was a crisis of the pastor's own making. He had forgotten to honor each part of Christ's ministry body. He was suffering from mission myopia.

I explained to the pastor that his ministry goals could be more effectively accomplished if he were to mobilize his board according to each person's unique personality. I encouraged him to ask his board for forgiveness and to repent of his judgmental attitude toward them. Several months later, I received an email from him; he had taken my advice to heart. After applying my recommendations, his relationship with his board was restored.

We should not be too critical of this pastor since we all tend do the same thing. We relate to, and understand best, the people-types who are most similar to ourselves. Our common values and interests quickly bind us together relationally. However when it comes to accomplishing a mission, it is essential that we incorporate the whole body of Christ. When we gather around us people who are just like ourselves, we sacrifice important perspectives and services that may be crucial to the mission that God has called us to accomplish.

Mission Myopia Influences Church Personalities

Mission myopia is so common among churches that the ministry temperaments of the dominant influencers within the ministry literally define the "personality" of the church organization. [Yes, as I mentioned earlier, churches and ministry organizations also have personalities, each with their own particular strengths and weaknesses.]

For example, one pastor had been able to identify his congregation's single biggest problem: Over its two-decade history, the church started many good programs, but had difficulty sustaining them. A simple assessment of the senior pastor and his board revealed that all the dominant leaders possessed *entrepreneurial* profiles—they were start-up people. No wonder they excelled at starting and failed at sustaining! The church leadership needed to identify two specific kinds of people within their congregation: those who could establish self-perpetuating ministry structures and those with *administrative* ability who were gifted at keeping programs going.

The personality of a ministry organization has a direct bearing on its ability to mobilize people for ministry and build effective ministry teams. In fact, the personality of a church often dictates who may serve within the ministry. In the church just mentioned, people with entrepreneurial temperaments easily found places of service, while others were clueless as to how to support the ministry. The principle of mission myopia—that people will naturally gather around others like themselves—inhibits other people-types from participating effectively within the ministry.

Often these disenfranchised Christ-followers feel like there simply is no place of ministry for them within their church. They may have tried earnestly to find a place that fits them, but in the end, feeling rejected and devalued, they ultimately leave the church. No healthy church leadership team intends to reject and devalue people, but it happens nonetheless.

Intentionally Modifying a Church Culture

Unlike human temperaments, which may mature but cannot be altered, organizational personalities can be intentionally modified to better facilitate God's mission for the church. Church culture modification is accomplished by recruiting and positioning the appropriate people-types, who possess the ministry temperaments the organization requires, into key positions of influence. The infusion of new leaders, with ministry temperaments that had previously been lacking within the leadership core, will over time dramatically transform the cultural personality of the organization.

The church which was able to establish many good ministry programs but unable to sustain them, needed to intentionally recruit and mobilize "managers" and "administrators" into positions of leadership. This process was far more emotionally difficult than it seemed at first. For two decades, the church's "start-up" culture had unconsciously viewed administrators and managers as non-relational "obstructionists," overly focused on task-oriented details.

> Church culture modification is accomplished by recruiting and positioning the appropriate people-types, who possess the ministry temperaments the organization requires, into key positions of influence.

As a result, most people with these ministry temperaments had left the church, and the few who remained were generally frustrated with their church leaders.

For the church to *change direction* (the definition of repentance), its leadership core needed to repent of their myopic values, the damage they had done to the church organization, and the emotional and spiritual harm they had inflicted upon those with ministry temperaments different than them. Such repentance required humility and an acknowledgement that the present church culture, as defined by the leadership core, would not allow the church to achieve God's ultimate purposes for the ministry. It also required them to risk significant cultural change—to step out in faith and include new leaders with different values.

As difficult as it is for individuals to repent, it can be even more difficult for organizations since the change of direction impacts many people, not just one. For this reason an organization's key influencers must agree that the proposed organizational changes are necessary if the ministry is to become more effective for Christ. Once agreement is reached, the key influencers must "put their hand to the plow and not look back" as they seek to implement the transformational strategy.

The difficult process of modifying a church's culture can be made easier with the following strategy:

First, recognize that it is always a top-down process. Begin with an evaluation of each key influencer's ministry temperament, at each functional layer within the organization. It is common in many churches to have three distinct leadership layers:

- Executive leadership (pastoral team)
- Support staff
- Lay leadership

Once you evaluate the results, you will likely discover that your organization displays a specific "temperament theme": a set of values shared by the key influencers. To determine an organization's temperament theme, begin by analyzing the actual scores within the four quadrants of each person's personality report (see the chart on the next page). Each assessment quadrant (i.e., *Relational Style, Information Style, Decision-making Style* and *Environmental Style*) contains two opposing values. For example, the *Relational Style* category scores individuals (or organizations) along a continuum that ranges from Independent to Social.

A temperament theme is defined in terms of "shared quadrant values" (*e.g.*, Independent vs. Social within the Relational personality quadrant) and not by the dominance of a specific ministry temperament (e.g., Protagonist) represented throughout the organization.

The Four Defining Personality Quadrants and Organizational Values

Relational Style

Independent < > Social

Your Relational Style determines how you relate to others, and whether you are energized by being with people, or need to be emotionally recharged by having time alone.

Information Assimilation Style

Abstract < > Concrete

Your Information Assimilation Style determines your information gathering preferences. An Abstract profile prefers concepts, ideas, theories, and philosophies. A Concrete profile prefers facts, tangible evidence, and proven methods.

Decision-Making Style

Head < > Heart

Your Decision-Making Style identifies whether your decisions are based more upon logic and facts (Head), or by perceptions and feelings (Heart).

Environmental Style

Systematic < > Adaptive

Your Environmental Style identifies how you relate to the world around you. Whether by trying to structure your world (Systematic), or are able to flex and flow with the demands of ever changing circumstances (Adaptive).

Relational Style:

Independent—
- Internalizes emotions and spiritual life
- Focus is upon the individual
- Emphasizes personal piety and service

Social—
- Highly relational community
- Focus is upon the group dynamic
- Emphasizes corporate piety and service

Decision-Making Style:

Head—
- Reliance upon information, facts and logic
- Prefers to implement proven ministry models
- Theologically emphasizes themes of guilt and grace

Heart—
- Considerate of people's feeling and perceptions
- Implements programs only when a consensus of support exists
- Theologically emphasizes themes of love and evangelism

Information Assimilation Style:

Abstract—
- Prefers ministry theories, theological concepts and experimentation
- An intellectually "open" community
- Typically a "teaching" church

Concrete—
- Prefers practical "real-life" concepts
- A community that focuses upon basic Christian faith and practice
- Typically a "programmed" church providing many felt-need services

Environmental Style:

Systematic—
- Prefers order and structure
- Organizational change is painful
- Services and programs are generally of high quality and well prepared

Adaptive—
- Prefers to "go with the flow"
- Organizational change is acceptable
- Services and program are generally of adequate quality, but may change often

Temperament themes define the culture of a church as it matures through the various phases of its development. The influencers within your ministry generally share one or more temperament themes. The simplest church model emphasizes a single temperament theme, typically the "Social" value from the *Relational Style* quadrant. As the church grows and its ministry requirements become more complex, church leaders unwittingly incorporate additional temperament themes at each stage. Although growth patterns will vary from church to church, this principle can be illustrated by walking through one common church growth scenario.

Stage 1: The Family-Feel Church

Churches typically develop in stages, according to their ability to incorporate and emphasize additional temperament themes within the four personality quadrants. A small church (at or below the 150-member barrier) will generally emphasize the *Relational Style* quadrant and uphold "Social" as their defining cultural value. At this stage in the ministry's development, the church functions much like a family with members who know and care for one another. There is little need for structure or programs.

Mission myopia is quite apparent in the Family-feel church. Relational people are highly valued and are attracted to the ministry, while systems-oriented and task-oriented people will generally wait out this phase of the church's development, hoping to influence the ministry as the church grows and matures. However if the church stagnates at the Family-Feel stage, people possessing ministry temperaments that value "Independence" may likely leave the ministry in erally internalize their emotions and thought process, prefer only a few deep relationships and tend to value mission-based tasks).

Stage 2: The Warm-Hearted Church

However, if the leadership of the Family-Feel church believes God is calling the ministry to grow beyond the family phase of development, the church will then need to adopt an additional quadrant-value that will compliment and expand upon their established social-relational value. Often the church leadership, without knowing it, will implement the *Decision-making Style* quadrant and seek to position decision-makers who have a high "Heart" value into positions of leadership. This new value adds a layer of organizational structure the ministry now requires and compliments the established social-relational culture. Since the current structures and programs are small and simple to manage at this stage, these relational leaders will excel until their ministry responsibilities grow in size and complexity. The church is now positioned to grow beyond the 150 barrier and will likely stagnate at approximately 500 people.

Mission myopia is now characterized by a high regard for people who are relational and make decisions based upon how they will impact others. People who relate differently, or make decisions differently, are often frustrated as they try to find a place of fit within the ministry organization. (People with a "Head" decision-making style prefer to utilize logic, facts and proven ministry models. They will likely be frustrated by the inefficiencies that are so common with leaders who possess a "Heart" decision-making style).

Stage 3: The Structured Church

The 500-person barrier represents the most significant cultural adjustment the church will have to make. At this stage the church organization will need to define program systems led by leaders who possess administrative and team-building skills. Administrative leaders are often imported from outside the ministry. (This is because highly relational values have dominated the church to this point, alienating task-oriented people and causing them to find a different church.) Without realizing it, the church leadership will adopt an additional cultural value found in the *Environmental Style* quadrant and seek to introduce into the established church culture a "Systematic" value.

At this point many relational people within the church begin to fear that the church is losing its "family-feel." Relationships are no longer defined in terms of the entire church body, but in the context of service and common interest subcultures, as well as shepherding small groups. The relational leaders they have known and loved are now being re-positioned or replaced by people with administrative and team-building abilities. (People with the "Adaptive" Environmental Style are likely able to make the emotional transition to the modified organizational culture, since they are generally able to flow with the various changes and challenges that impact their life.)

I recently observed a 450-member church struggling with the difficult adjustment from Warm-hearted to Structured. Its children's ministry was led by a director who possessed a protagonist ministry temperament. The protagonist ministry temperament is quite charismatic when in front of people and thrives in a non-structured environment. The protagonist is not skilled as an administrator or team builder. While this ministry temperament likely served the children's ministry well in the early stages of its development, the non-structured culture was now impeding the children's ministry from growing into excellence.

The people who valued "winging it" rather than planning and preparation were able to function within the various roles required by the children's ministry. However, people with ministry temperaments that valued administration, team-building, planning and preparation could not fit within the "wing-it" culture defined by the protagonist leader. If the children's ministry was to reach the next level of development, the protagonist culture needed to be replaced or modified.

The ministry temperaments required to take the children's ministries program to the next level (*i.e.*, administrators and team leaders) were the very people-types that the established culture had, until now, been alienating. (A protagonist's "wing-it" values can always find a place of service within a structured, team-based culture. However, a structured, team-based person can rarely find a place of service within the protagonist's "wing-it" culture.)

When a Warm-hearted church is able to transition to a Structured church, and include people who identify with and can implement the new "systematic" cultural value within the church, a new army of systems-oriented people will be unleashed to serve within the church. These people have not known how to fit and serve effectively in the Family-feel or Warm-hearted church. But now a new team-based synergy liberates strategic planners, administrators, managers and team leaders into places of effective ministry. The Structured church will thrive until it reaches approximately 1,500 people.

Mission myopia at this stage of development occurs on two distinct and divisive fronts: The old guard values relational people and resists the inclusion of other ministry temperaments. Similarly, the new guard relates best to systems-oriented people. The unfortunate consequence is often the creation of a culture gap that may take years for the church to overcome. Often the adjustment is made by sacrificing a significant number of relational people to other smaller churches and replacing them with new systems people.

Sacrificing people is never God's ideal. No one ministry temperament is superior to another—we all need each other. However, our roles will inevitably change as the organizational personality dynamics change.

Stage 4: The Hierarchical Church

The Structured church transitions into a Hierarchical church when it consolidates top-tier authority structures, while at the same time integrating a new quadrant value: the "Concrete" value found within the *Information Assimilation* style quadrant. The ministry now focuses upon providing many concrete and practical ministry services.

Generally, there is a unifying thematic value that binds these many services together. Common unifying themes include: Outreach, Seeker-targeted, Seeker-sensitive, Life Purpose, Global Impact, etc. Because of the complex network of team-based ministries, literally thousands of people of all ministry temperaments can find a place of service and rise up in status and influence within the ranks. (The Abstract personality value may dominate in a large church that is seeking to devise and implement innovative ministry paradigms. These are the cutting-edge ministries that define the ministry models that other mainstream churches imitate.)

Relationships are now nurtured in the context of membership within a ministry team, joining with others around a common interest, or through participation in a small group. In recent years the trend has been to break the Hierarchical church down into small functional and relational units. This process has given rise to regional satellite churches—one church meeting concurrently in various locations, via Internet streaming from the mother church.

Mission myopia occurs when the ministry tends to value and promote the elite leaders. These leaders-of-leaders excel at team building, administration and team motivation. People who do not possess the same level of administrative and team building skill as the elite leaders may feel inferior or devalued. Often the level of excellence demanded by the Hierarchical church permits only the paid "experts" to serve in visible roles.

With the new millennium, a post-modern reaction to the modernist Hierarchical church has given birth to the house church and various other emergent church movements. These movements aspire to recapture the relational intimacy and spiritual experientialism that many people feel have been lost within the Hierarchical church. However, these movements in essence are simply starting the church-growth cycle over again by forming post-modern versions of the "Family-feel" church!

Conclusion

It is impossible for any church to perfectly balance all the opposing values in each personality quadrant. If this "perfect" balance could be found, then all churches would simply be clones of one another and so would look alike, function alike, and serve alike. The goal of cultural modification is not to make every church alike. Rather, the goal is to allow diverse ministry temperaments to play appropriate and supportive roles within the ministry's unique mission and organizational development. Those ministry temperaments that have been kept outside of positions of influence within the organization may indeed provide the exact values, insights and resources the ministry requires to mature to the next level.

For individual Christ-followers, this cultural modification process will require patience as they support their leaders with prayer and godly counsel. You can also support your leaders by applying the following suggestions:

- Don't be a part of the problem by practicing mission myopia within your personal ministry.
- If you feel you do not fit within your church, try to be a part of the solution by helping church leadership understand that mission myopia may be restricting your ability to serve. Do not be quick to "pack up and leave." It is likely that God has placed you at your church for the purpose of broadening and deepening its ministry impact.
- Understand that God has called you to serve Him in the context of the body of Christ. Rarely does God call us to serve as spiritual "lone rangers." After all, even the Lone Ranger had Tonto!

The Ministry Personality Assessment

Most every ministry suffers from "mission myopia"—a cultural preference for particular ministry temperaments. As a result, a church ministry generally develops a distinct personality that promotes particular values and styles to the exclusion of other necessary values and styles. The brief assessment tool below will provide your ministry leaders and laity with a broad understanding of your ministry's current cultural strengths and weaknesses and the impact those strengths and weaknesses may have upon the development of healthy ministry teams. To take the assessment, please visit www.assessme.org/extra.

Organizational Personality Worksheet

A. Our Organizational Personality: _____

_____

B. I affirm that my ministry organization possesses the following STRENGTHS:

1. _____
2. _____
3. _____
4. _____
5. _____

C. I affirm that my ministry organization possesses the following WEAKNESSES:

1. _____
2. _____

Chapter 4

Godly Passion

Our ministry temperament determines how we approach the world around us and interpret our daily experiences. It also causes us to be attracted to certain experiences and disinterested in others. As a result we all develop unique patterns of interests, passions and skills.

One of my most awesome privileges as a father of two young children is watching the personalities of my children emerge. I have a son, Joshua, and an older daughter, Alyssa, and they could not be more different.

Joshua is an aggressive, competitive, critical analyzer of details. One day when he was five years old, he emerged from the closet in my office with a box and asked what it was. When I told him it was a chess training set and asked if he wanted to learn how to play, he responded enthusiastically—and so the chess lessons began. In a matter of weeks, I was being humiliated by a kindergartner as he began to beat me at almost every game.

Joshua was so passionate about chess that he played it

every day. If nobody was available to play with him, he would play by himself—both sides of the board. When he learned about regional and state tournaments, he wanted to compete. In the two years that followed, Joshua won a trophy at every tournament he attended.

Where did Joshua get this skill and passion? It is innate in his personality. His personality drives him toward certain activities and away from others.

In contrast, my daughter Alyssa is a gentle-spirited girl who loves reading, spending time with friends and riding horses. On a recent vacation we had an opportunity to take Alyssa to watch an equestrian competition. I was confident that this event would be the highlight of her vacation. However within thirty minutes she was bored. At first I didn't understand why she did not enjoy the event, but after talking with her it became clear: it was a "competition." Unlike Joshua, Alyssa devalues competition and prefers relational harmony. She would have preferred to spend the afternoon hanging out in the stables and talking with the people who owned the horses.

Career Perspective vs. Mission Perspective

Our personality type was given to us by our Creator to be used for His service, and it inspires, to a large extent, our field of potential interests. Over time, and with exploration, certain dominant interests emerge as passions, and with greater experience, our passions form into skills. There is a direct line between our interests, passions and skills. But how do these dynamics relate to our potential ministry mission?

It is natural for people to look at their passions and skills as markers pointing them toward a career path. However, as Christ-followers, it is more important that we interpret our passions and skills as markers intended to direct us to the work our Lord desires to accomplish through us.

This reminds me of the true meaning of the word "vocation." It comes from the Latin word *invocatio,* which is translated, "To call upon God for help." Somehow we have twisted the meaning of "vocation" from something *God accomplishes through us* to something *we do for a living.*

> As Christ-followers, it is more important that we interpret our passions and skills as pointers intended to direct us to the kind of ministry work our Lord desires to accomplish through us.

If you really want to fulfill your divine mission in this world, however, I believe a mental, emotional and spiritual paradigm shift is required. You need to reorient your thinking and priorities around a life emphasis upon *invocatio*—passionately seeking to discover what God desires to accomplish through you! God's revelation will then drive all your life's priorities, including those involving career decisions.

When a boy who has always displayed a high degree of mechanical aptitude becomes an adult, he may choose to become a mechanic. Is being a mechanic his life mission? Well, it depends. Did he choose to serve as a mechanic simply to earn an income? Or did he allow God to guide his decision-making process, and reveal to him where and how he would best advance the Kingdom of Christ as a mechanic? His perspective and priorities are the factors determining whether he merely has a secular vocation or a mission-focused *invocatio.*

The fundamental issue before us is whether our passions and skills will be used to serve our own ambitions or the ambitions of Christ. The table below illustrates the dichotomy between the common career perspective and a Biblically inspired mission perspective:

Career Perspective	Mission Perspective
• **Primary Goal:** Making money • **Primary Focus:** Use my abilities to meet my needs and the needs of my family • **Success Is Measured:** By social status and financial independence • **Faith Focus:** Self-reliance	• **Primary Goal:** Making disciples of Christ • **Primary Focus:** Use my abilities to serve God and the needs of others • **Success Is Measured:** By whether I have been obedient to God's leading and empowerment • **Faith Focus:** Reliance upon the Holy Spirit

God truly desires to accomplish a significant ministry through each one of us. Our personality, and subsequent interests, passions and skills are all intended to point us in the direction of that mission. That significant mission may be accomplished in the context of full-time ministry or lay ministry service, or while serving as *salt and light* within a secular context (Matt. 5:13–16).

> Somehow, we have twisted the meaning of "vocation" from something God accomplishes through us to something we do for a living.

It is important that we consult God earnestly regarding His desired path for our lives and not simply assume that we should enter the secular arena. I find it curious that most Christ-followers assume that they should follow a secular career path unless God calls them into a different direction. Rather, should we not assume that God has called us and set us apart for His service and simply ask Him where and how.

I already hear the voices of skeptics ringing in my ears: "But let's be practical. I have a family and obligations—I need to make a living!" Don't you think that God knows these things? Do you recall what Jesus told His disciples when He sent them out into the mission field for the first time?

> Freely you have received, freely give. Do not take along any gold or silver or copper in your belts; take no bag for the journey, or extra tunic, or sandals or a staff; for the worker is worth his keep. (Matt. 10:8–10)

You are God's worker, and you are "worth your keep." If God is calling you to utilize the interests, passions and skills He has developed in you to accomplish a God-empowered *invocatio*, then He will provide all you require to accomplish His will. This is a difficult faith-lesson for many Christ-followers to learn. Yet we must be careful not to allow our lack of faith to erect obstacles that will impede or limit God's ability to accomplish His work through us. While we all are imperfect in faith, should not our prayer be: "I do believe; help me overcome my unbelief" (Mark 9:24)?

This point was vividly illustrated for me one summer when I took my family to the beach on Lake Michigan for a "day of rest." While at the beach we encountered a friend from a ministry where we had previously served. It was so good to see him again and to catch up with what was going on in his life. As we talked it became clear that he was miserable in his job.

He held a very lucrative position in an international organization, but the company had continued to cut and slash positions. His division now employed only a fraction of the people it once possessed; yet the company was expecting the same results as before the cuts took place. My friend was obviously stressed, frustrated and tired.

Apart from his job, my friend is a highly creative person who absolutely excels at ministering to children. I asked him, "If you could do anything you wanted in life, what would it be?" He responded that he would love to run a Christian camp for children. So I asked why he didn't pursue this passion.

He responded sadly, "Because any camp director position would pay half the salary that I am currently making."

I feel for my friend. He has a big, beautiful home and a high-paying job. Yet not only is he miserable, he is also potentially limiting his mission impact in this world—all for the sake of money! My friend would indeed be an outstanding camp director or children's ministry director. He is perfectly suited for such ministry roles. His personality is ideal for working with children, and his ability to communicate creatively is nothing short of phenomenal! He is passionate about ministering to children and exudes strong leadership abilities.

To my friend's credit, he does lead the children's ministry in his church as a volunteer. But I cannot help but feel that God has much more in store for him, if he could only come to the point of trusting the Holy Spirit for help and financial support rather than an international corporation.

Within my own my marriage and ministry life, my wife Tamara and I have often wrestled with the question of how each of us is called to serve the Lord. Tamara is a highly gifted woman, with a Bachelor of Arts in education and a master's degree in communication. She also deeply values ministering to children, especially her own. It has always been my ambition to support my wife and family so that Tamara could invest in our children and her ministry with other kids. However, we have both discovered that God's plans are often quite different from our own.

For years I had an overwhelming feeling that God was calling me to develop Internet tools that would enable churches to extend their disciple-making and ministry-mobilization efforts online. This "calling" seemed to be in conflict with my responsibility to provide for my family because to develop such tools would take several years and hundreds of thousands of dollars. I would not be able to receive a salary sufficient to support my family for at least three to five years. I tried to devise a way to earn a full-time salary and work on my "calling" part-time, but God closed each door I tried.

In the course of our struggle to discern God's leading, a ministry friend by the name of Dan Webster suggested that Tamara and I fly to Oregon and spend several days in a Life Planning session with Tom Patterson, a godly and gifted strategic planner and author of *Living the Life You Were Meant To Live* (Thomas Nelson, 1982). God used our meetings with Tom to confirm that my vision for developing online ministry systems was truly His calling for my life and that the time demands of this ministry required my full-time commitment and focus.

God impressed upon Tamara's heart that He wanted her

to support my calling. This meant that she would have to take the lead in providing for our family financially until the ministry was self-supporting. She consequently began working full-time for an international corporation.

Both Tamara and I firmly believe that her "calling" to work full-time is only temporary. We remain confident that God has far greater things in store for her life and ministry. Yet she has been willing to make this sacrifice because she views her role as an *invocatio* that enables her husband to provide online ministry resources to churches across the world. I am eternally grateful for Tamara and for her sacrificial heart that has allowed us to pursue God's calling together as husband and wife.

It is one thing to identify our various interests, skills and passions. It is another to discern how God is directing us to use them in daily life. The Biblically based "Mission Perspective" will inspire us to evaluate four values-based questions:

1. What is my primary goal? (*i.e.*, making disciples of Christ)
2. What is my primary focus? (*i.e.*, using my abilities to serve the needs of others)
3. How will I measure success? (*i.e.*, by whether I have been obedient to God's leading and empowerment)
4. What is my faith focus? (*i.e.*, reliance upon the Holy Spirit)

What interests, passions and skills has God given you? Take a few moments to reflect upon your life, and see if you can discover developmental patterns that will shed light on the nature of your ministry mission.

The Passion Assessment

For each phase of your life, identify the top three interest areas that dominated that life phase. Once you have completed your listings, please carefully respond to the application questions.

Childhood: Ages 0–12
- Interest #1 _____
- Interest #2 _____
- Interest #3 _____

Teen Years: Ages 13–18
- Interest #1 _____
- Interest #2 _____
- Interest #3 _____

Young Adult: Ages 19–30
- Interest #1 _____
- Interest #2 _____
- Interest #3 _____

Adult: Ages 31–Present
- Interest #1 _____
- Interest #2 _____
- Interest #3 _____

Application

Once you have completed your listings of interests, respond to the following questions:

A. Interests: Are you able to identify a common interest theme that has followed you throughout the various phases of your life?

_____

_____

_____

_____

_____

_____

B. Passions: Have any of your interests emerged as life-passions? A passion can be identified as a dominant interest that preoccupies your time or thoughts.

_____

_____

_____

_____

_____

C. Skills: What skills have you developed over the years because of your primary interests and passions?

_____

_____

_____

_____

_____

D. Satisfaction: Name one or two activities that, upon reflection, gave you the greatest sense of joy and personal satisfaction. What interests, passions or skills were utilized during those events?

_____

_____

_____

_____

_____

_____

E. Experience: Have you observed God using any of your passions or skills through personal ministry already? If so, how?

_____

_____

_____

_____

_____

_____

F. Motivation: Do you have a growing awareness of God's *invocatio*—what He wishes to accomplish through you—using your primary interests, passions and skills? If so, consider the following questions:

1. If my primary goal is making disciples of Christ, then how do I perceive that my interests, passions and skills can be used to facilitate that process?

_____

_____

_____

_____

2. If my primary focus is using my abilities to serve the needs of others, then how do I perceive that my interests, passions and skills can be used to facilitate that process?

_____

_____

_____

_____

3. If I measure success by whether I have been obedient to God's leading and empowerment, then how do I perceive God is leading me to use my interests, passions and skills?

_____

_____

_____

_____

_____

_____

4. If my faith-focus is reliance upon the Holy Spirit, then what faith challenges do I anticipate I will face? How does God want me to respond?

_____

_____

_____

_____

_____

The Passion Puzzle

You have just taken a few moments to reflect upon your life and have noted specific areas of interest, passions and skills that have defined your existence since birth. When were you most passionate? What were you passionate about? Did your passion ever drive you to accomplish anything of significance?

I am convinced that the people who are most satisfied with their lives, and have accomplished the most, are those who have identified their dominant life-passions and are using those passions to serve others.

Impassioned people overcome obstacles, risk failure and demand to make a difference in this world. You and I cannot help but be inspired by the passion of great leaders like Martin Luther King when he said, "I have a dream." Passion is naturally infectious; when expressed purposefully, it can quickly spread to others.

Passion is a natural human attribute. This is because our God, who is passionate about us, burned His passion into our DNA. Yes, God is passionate! He is passionate about you! He is passionate about overcoming sin in this world! He is passionate about taking joy in His creation! When we live passionately, we live life to the fullest and in so doing we emulate the passion of our Father-Creator.

Yet many of us have been taught to restrain our passions. For some reason passionate living is viewed as too extreme—especially in traditional, respectable church culture. Instead we find ourselves vicariously living out our passion through the books we read and the movies we see. When was the last time you saw a movie about a character who lived a safe and practical life? Never! Such a movie would be a total flop. We innately sense that we were created by God to somehow resemble the movie characters we admire.

Inside each of us is a passionate hero or heroine striving to be unleashed. I believe it is possible to unleash the hero within us if only we have the courage and faith in Christ to take the risks required to really make a difference in this world—and, more importantly, a difference for the kingdom of Christ!

The passion which is directed toward God and driven by His Spirit will consistently display the four dynamics found in Second Timothy 1:7: "For God did *not* give us [1] *a spirit of timidity*, but [2] *a spirit of power*, [3] *of love* and [4] *of self-discipline.*"

1. *A fearless (not timid) spirit*: Our faith in God's leadership and empowerment is evident in our boldness, confidence and assurance.
2. *Empowerment from the Spirit*: The Holy Spirit enables us to accomplish what He calls us to do in such a manner that God receives the credit, not us.
3. *A spirit of love*: We have a sincere desire to express Christ's love to others or to enable others to express Christ's love. This love is characterized by humble service and self-sacrifice.
4. *A sober (self-disciplined) spirit*: Our lives display discipline and sound judgment regarding the task at hand, along with daily dependence upon the Holy Spirit.

We can illustrate these dynamics in what I call the *Passion Puzzle*. If any one piece of the puzzle is lacking, we should consider: a) whether our mission-passion is truly from the Holy Spirit, b) whether we perceive God's timing correctly and c) whether we are yet fully prepared for the mission.

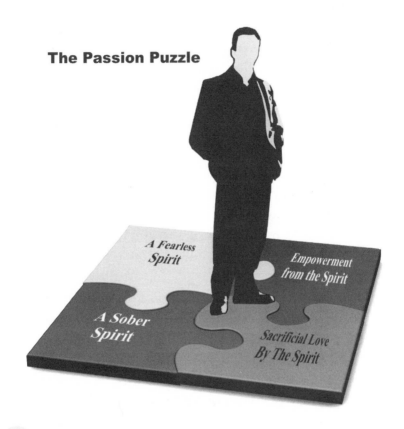

The Passion Puzzle

A Fearless Spirit

Empowerment from the Spirit

A Sober Spirit

Sacrificial Love By The Spirit

The Impact of Missing Pieces

- If we have a passion for ministry but *lack the faith* to step out and trust the Holy Spirit's leading each step of the way, we will find our mission immobilized by all the obstacles that Satan will construct along the path.

- If we have a passion for ministry but *lack the empowerment of the Holy Spirit*, we will find our mission immobilized by our personal limitations and imperfections.
- If we have a passion for ministry but *do not serve Christ and others from a spirit of sacrificial love*—willing to sacrifice personal time, energy, money and resources for the benefit of others—then our efforts are likely based upon selfish ambition and pride; our "ministry" is just a "resounding gong or clanging cymbal" (1 Cor. 13:1).
- If we have a passion for ministry but *do not display a sober spirit* evidenced by self-discipline and a dependency upon the Holy Spirit, then we likely chase after dreams and fantasies, and not Kingdom realities.

When one or more of the Passion Puzzle pieces is lacking in our life and mission, no amount of human passion can be a substitute. Spirit-inspired passion is unstoppable. When God calls us to a mission and His Spirit is allowed to lead us, we are then in a position to be used by Him and to see Him display His glory in incredible ways.

I was once asked by a sincere Christ-follower why we don't see God working today as depicted in the New Testament. My response was simple: All too often, we want God to work *for* us, rather than positioning our life to allow God to work *through* us. People who are fearful, self-sufficient, self-obsessed dreamers will not see God work miracles through them until they first allow Him to work his miracle of life-transformation (sanctification) in them.

A Fearless Spirit

I find it interesting that Mel Gibson named his movie *The Passion of Christ*. Christ's passion for us motivated Him to endure torture and crucifixion so that our relationship with God might be restored. In fact, look closely at the language Christ Himself uses to describe the mission to which we are called: "From the days of John the Baptist until now, the kingdom of heaven has been forcefully advancing, and forceful men lay hold of it" (Matt. 11:12).

The Greek word translated here as "forceful" can only be properly understood by its greater context. It can have either an active or a passive meaning.[1] In this passage Jesus promises us that we will both be victorious (active) and we will suffer (passive). The kind of "forceful" people that Jesus was talking about recognize that God will ensure their ultimate victory. However, they also realize that the victory will only be attained through suffering—your mission will not be easy!

> All too often, we want God to work for us, rather than positioning our life to allow God to work through us.

Are you a "forceful" man or woman? Are you impassioned to help the kingdom of Christ forcefully advance? The Spirit of Christ calls us to live fearlessly in our moments of victory as well as in our moments of suffering. Now is not the time to cower in passivity. Now is not the time for "practical" living. Now is the time to "press on and take hold of that for which Christ Jesus took hold of [us]. . . . Forgetting what is behind and straining toward what is ahead, [we] press on toward the goal to win the prize for which God has called [us] heavenward in Christ Jesus" (Phil. 3:12–14).

Empowerment from the Spirit

We cannot accomplish this mission in our own strength. When Jesus was nearing the end of His mission on earth, He told His disciples that they would receive power to be God's witnesses once they received the Holy Spirit (Acts 1:8). Consider for a moment the disciples of Jesus and their remarkable transformation from cowards to "forceful men."

When Jesus was betrayed in Gethsemane, all the disciples fled—one man even ran away naked in his attempt to escape! Later that night, Peter denied knowing Jesus on three separate occasions (Mark 14). After Jesus died, the disciples cowered in a locked room together for fear of the Jews (John 20:19). Only days later, on the day of Pentecost, these cowards were suddenly transformed into "forceful" men and women who boldly proclaimed Christ in the open streets and defied the religious leaders who had condemned Christ. The transformation was only made possible by the empowerment and indwelling of the Holy Spirit.

When you received Christ as your Savior, you did so by the work of the Holy Spirit, who drew you to Him and granted you faith to believe in Him. However, it becomes so easy for those who have come to Christ by the Spirit to then serve Him by the flesh—their own human effort. For most of us, true dependence upon the Holy Spirit is only possible when we come to the end of our abilities—when the mission demands more than we have to give. It is at that point that we are forced to make a decision. Either we give up and walk away, or we choose to persevere in faith and allow the Holy Spirit to carry us through to the completion of our mission.

One night I was discussing this very subject with my nine-year-old daughter Alyssa as I put her to bed. I was trying to explain to her the old Christian saying "Where God guides, He provides." She was having difficulty understanding how God actively provides for His people. So I encouraged Alyssa to pretend that God offered her a million dollars.

"Now," I challenged, "God could hand over to you the entire amount at one time, but then would you really need to trust Him in your day-to-day life"?

She answered, "No."

Then I challenged her again, "What if God offered you a million dollars, and all He asked was that you trust Him to give you the exact amounts of money you needed, when you needed it. The money is still yours—what is the difference?"

Alyssa responded: "I would need to trust that God would give me the money He promised."

"Exactly," I said. "You have to trust in the character of God to provide for you, and as He proves faithful to provide for you, your faith in His good and loving character grows and you are able to trust Him for even greater things."

Sadly, many Christians fail in their mission because they don't respond in faith to the many opportunities to trust God that come their way. The accomplishment of your mission is impossible without true faith; in the same manner, "without faith it is impossible to please God, because anyone who comes to him must believe that he exists and that he rewards those who earnestly seek him" (Heb. 11:6). It is easy to believe that God exists, but it is contrary to our independent nature to "earnestly seek" Him and even more difficult for us to trust Him for the "rewards" He has in store for our life and ministry.

Always remember this: since nothing is impossible for God, the only factor limiting the scope and impact of your mission is your faith in God. Let Christ be the Author and Finisher of your faith (Heb. 12:2), and nothing will keep God from accomplishing great things through you.

A Spirit of Love

When the Holy Spirit fell upon the disciples, the Spirit began to lead them into "all truth" (John 16:12) regarding Christ. They were finally able to accept Jesus not simply as their Teacher, nor only as their Savior, but also as their living Lord.

There is a fundamental distinction between relating to Jesus as "Savior" and as "Lord." Immature Christ-followers often relate to Jesus as their Savior because as Savior, Jesus is the Servant of humanity—and after all, we all like to be served! A mature Christ-follower, however, learns that Jesus also expects that we will learn to relate to Him as our Lord.

Lordship implies that Christ is the Master and we are His servants. In modern terms, He is our Boss. The Boss is in charge. Yet unlike our human bosses, who motivate us by their demands, the Spirit of Christ motivates us to serve Him by His love for us. This is why the Apostle Paul is able to proclaim, "Christ's love compels us" (2 Cor. 5:14).

Love is indeed compelling. I love my wife Tamara passionately. Although I loved her from the moment I first met her and knew that she was the one God had selected for me, Tamara did not quickly arrive at the same conclusion. She needed some convincing.

Early in our dating relationship, I discovered that one of her interests was rollerblading, something I had never tried. Without her knowledge, I rented the necessary equipment and practiced all weekend, then called her to ask for an "impromptu" date. I don't know if I have ever made a bigger fool of myself than on that date with Tamara. I wiped out repeatedly and even ran into a few parked cars!

Love indeed compels us—to the point that we will do what we have never done before to gain what we've never had before. (And yes, I did get the girl!)

Similarly, because of Christ's love for us, His passion drove Him to the cross (1 Cor. 1:18). But Christ's passion for us did not stop at the cross. The cross was the launching point for Christ's universal mission, as well as the launching point for His calling upon our lives.

> But because of his great love for us, God, who is rich in mercy, made us alive with Christ even when we were dead in our transgressions—it is by grace you have been saved. And God raised us up with Christ and seated us with him in the heavenly realms in Christ Jesus, in order that in the coming ages he might show the incomparable riches of his grace, expressed in his kindness to us in Christ Jesus. For it is by grace you have been saved, through faith—and this [faith] is not from yourselves, it is the gift of God—not of works, so that no one can boast. *For we are God's workmanship, created in Christ Jesus to do good works, which God prepared in advance for us to do.* (Eph. 2:4–10)

What is our appropriate response to the love that Christ has lavished on us? It is to accomplish the mission (good works) which He ordained for us. How can we do any less?

God has offered us the riches of His love, a place in His eternal kingdom and a life in this world that possesses an incredible mission purpose! His love is indeed compelling. The more you and I mature in our love-relationship with Christ, the more we will be compelled to become the "forceful" men and women He always intended us to be.

A Sober Spirit

There is a significant difference between a passionate person who "chases after the wind," and a passion-inspired person who pursues earnestly God's calling upon his or her life. A sober spirit (Greek: *sophronew*) is characterized by self-discipline, a humble attitude and reliance upon the Holy Spirit. Different Bible translations render this word as follows:

- "Self-Discipline" (New International Version)
- "Sound Mind" (King James Version)
- "Soberness" (Wycliffe New Testament)
- "Wise Discretion" (Darby Translation)
- "Self-Control" (English Standard Version)

Sophronew carries with it a sense of "mental health." From God's perspective, sin has caused us to literally go insane. Romans 8:7 tells us that the sinful mind is hostile to God and cannot submit to God. Until we come into a faith relationship with Jesus, our minds are entirely polluted by sin, and our ability to think clearly is entirely corrupted by sin. Our minds seek only to gratify and glorify self. However, God desires that we start to think correctly about who we are in relation to Christ and our proper place in this world.

This is why the Apostle Paul tells us that we must receive a "brain-transplant." If we are to have any hope of serving Christ faithfully, we must "renew" our minds—get a new mind and a new way of thinking—so that we will not "conform any longer to the pattern of this world, but be transformed . . . able to test and approve what God's will is—his good, pleasing and perfect will" (Rom. 12:2). This mind renewal is an ongoing, lifelong process that can only take place when we "set our mind on what the Spirit desires" (Rom. 8:5–6) and give up control over our lives.

When I was a senior in high school, I would have called myself a Christian, but I was often not living as a Christian should. One night I was drinking with my girlfriend, and though I don't remember doing this, apparently I downed an entire fifth of vodka. I passed out and stopped breathing. I had to be rushed to the hospital by ambulance.

When I woke up the next day in the emergency room, I was scared. I did not know what had happened. Had we been in a car accident? Was my girlfriend all right? The doctor came in to the room to talk with me.

"Young man, you had better take a hard look at your life. I have no medical explanation for why you are still alive. The amount of alcohol in your body could have killed someone twice your weight."

God in His mercy had spared my life. I realized at that moment that running my life my way was destroying me. That day in the hospital room, I rededicated my life to Christ. That decision initiated a sequence of life-changing events, the most important of which was that I began to communicate with God and study the Bible earnestly every day.

Through this process, God began to renew my mind so that I could think according to His will and purposes. This mind-renewal process began to change my life priorities from valuing selfish ambition to valuing the kingdom of Christ. My personal passion had once been to become a corporate lawyer, make a lot of money, drive a 7–series BMW and live in a big house on Lake Michigan. God has now transformed my passion/vision for my life's mission into a desire to have the greatest impact I can for the kingdom of Christ while on this planet.

Phases of Passion Confirmation

I believe there are three kinds of passionate people: *dreamers*, *visionaries*, and *missionaries*. A *dreamer* wishes the world were different. The *visionary* understands how the world could be made different. The *missionary* makes a difference in the world.

> There are three kinds of passionate people: Dreamers, Visionaries and Missionaries. A Dreamer wishes the world were different. The Visionary understands how the world could be made different. The Missionary makes a difference in the world.

In some respects, before any "missionary" is able to make a difference in the world, they must first move through the developmental phases from dream to vision, and from vision to mission. As they pass through each phase, they should seek confirmation that they are proceeding down a path that is indeed God's will. This confirmation must come first from God and secondly from godly people.

Prospective missionaries should not expect everyone to affirm them, however. Not everyone values dreams. Many people have difficulty perceiving intangible visions. And the majority fear the risks associated with true mission.

In the case of E-Church Essentials, I found that family members and ministry leaders who were over forty years of age had difficulty understanding the Internet and technology culture associated with our unique ministry venture. I soon learned to differentiate between my need for "confirmation" versus "affirmation." *Confirmation* is an objective need to validate the ministry mission—whether the mission is from God, in God's timing and being accomplished in God's way. *Affirmation*, on the other hand, is an emotional need to validate one's self-worth.

When I shared my vision with various people, and watched them respond either positively or critically, I had to be careful not to take their words too personally. When I felt hurt or injured by someone's response, I realized that I had moved away from the realm of "confirmation" of the ministry mission and into the realm of "affirmation" of me as a person.

With this distinction in mind, let's explore the three developmental phases that all people encounter in their desire to confirm their passion for ministry.

The Dreamer Stage

At the "dreamer" stage God gives birth to an idea. God enables us to see the world through new lenses, which allows us to perceive a problem and consider the possibilities and potential for how we can participate in providing a solution.

Unfortunately, many people never move beyond the dream and take steps to make that dream a reality.

I once planted a church in a town characterized by spiritual dysfunction, including broken homes, absentee fathers, poverty and illiteracy. Often well-meaning people in the church would offer up their dreams for the kinds of ministry that could be accomplished in this town.

One man, noting the absence of spiritually healthy male influences, suggested that we should start a "Free Christian Boys Camp," where Christian men could invest into the boys of this town. I told him I thought this was an excellent idea and suggested that he begin researching how we could make it happen. And there the dream died.

Many dreams die on the bed of good intentions. It takes more than a good idea and wishful thinking; it takes conviction that the dream is from God and a faith commitment to take the dream to the next level.

The Vision Stage

Dreamers who possess the necessary conviction and commitment are motivated to understand God's strategy for turning the dream into a vision. They must develop a vision-plan.

When God gave me the dream to develop E-Church Essentials, I proceeded to meet with many visionary pastors, consultants and strategic planners over the course of 18 months, seeking counsel on how best to turn God's dream into a workable vision. I felt that two key questions needed to be answered:

1. Was my dream a valid ministry need. If so, how best should this need be addressed?
2. Was I the right person to be the "missionary" for this project?

Through these conversations (which culminated in a three-day consultation with Tom Patterson in Oregon) God helped me to formulate a plan and provided me with the confirmation I required. In the months that followed, He provided additional confirmation: the financial and human resources needed to take the vision-plan to the next level—a ministry mission.

The Missionary Stage

The final stage of confirmation is the transformation of visionaries into missionaries. Up to this point very little faith has been required. A dream requires little faith; a vision, maybe a bit more. However, once God makes it known to us that it is time to step out and begin serving according to His leading, we take our first real steps of faith. We trust that God has inspired our dream, has directed our vision and is leading us into our mission. Now begins the grand adventure of faith.

The Apostle Paul tells us that God is "able to do immeasurably more than all we ask or imagine, according to his power that is at work within us" (Eph. 3:20). I am sure that all of us can imagine some extreme things and pray some extreme prayers. Yet it is likely that we still dream too small and expect of God too little.

One fundamental challenge that confronts all Christ-followers is that of seeking to compact our mission into something we can manage. If we succeed then we may no longer wait upon God for His empowerment. A God-driven mission is never one that we are capable of handling ourselves.

In fact, Ephesians 3:20 tells us that the only real responsibility you and I have is to "imagine" and "ask" in such a manner that we cannot help but be dependent upon God's working in us and through us to accomplish His good purposes. When God shows up and does His work, we receive the ultimate confirmation that He has indeed blessed the mission. The converse is also true. When we compact our mission into something we can manage, we deprive ourselves of experiencing God's empowerment and confirmation.

The Important Role of Passion Confirmation

Confirmation can take the form of human affirmation, as ministry leaders affirm the spiritual fruit that our ministry efforts have produced. It also comes as we are trained and equipped by ministry mentors, and they are able to affirm our gifts, abilities and preparation for ministry. Does all confirmation look alike? Is it only displayed through God's miraculous intervention or human affirmation? No. In fact, it can resemble a spiritual wilderness experience, a lonely struggle to trust God as we pursue the dream He has given us—especially when all evidence suggests that the dream may never become reality.

Confirmation in the Wilderness

I remember listening to a radio interview with Frank Perretti, a Christian author. He recounted how he believed God had called him to be a pastor but that his pastoral experience appeared to be a miserable failure. He lost his pastoral position and was forced to work for twelve years in a fiberglass factory making skis. Only after twelve years of wandering in his spiritual desert did Frank Perretti finally begin to move into his true ministry mission as a Christian author.

Was Frank Perretti called to be a pastor? Yes, but not in the traditional sense. Through his books, Frank Perretti has pastored millions of people across the planet. God wanted to do "immeasurably more than [Frank] could ask or imagine"! God simply needed to reshape his dream, reshape his vision—and probably reshape Frank Perretti himself—for the true mission God intended for him.

Did his "wilderness wanderings" mean that Frank was not being confirmed by God? Absolutely not! In fact, I would suggest just the opposite. Seldom does God use people in a significant way without first testing and purifying their faith, and humbling their hearts, through wilderness experiences. The wilderness experience is a time of preparation. To that end, the wilderness experience itself is confirmation of our calling to serve Christ.

In the forty years that the people of Israel wandered in the wilderness, God daily confirmed that they were His covenant people. He provided manna for them to eat and water for them to drink. God made sure that their sandals and clothes did not wear out over the course of forty years. Had the Israelites not experienced God's daily provision through their wilderness wanderings, it is unlikely that the next generation would have had sufficient faith to enter into the Promised Land.

Even the Apostle Paul's ministry was confirmed through a spiritual wilderness experience. Paul gives us a glimpse into his preparation for ministry in Galatians 1:15–17:

But when God, who set me apart from birth and called me by his grace, was pleased to reveal his Son in me so that I might preach him among the Gentiles, I did not consult any man, nor did I go up to Jerusalem to see those who were apostles before I was, but I went immediately into Arabia and later returned to Damascus.

Paul endured his wilderness experience, ministering alone in the deserts of Arabia for many years, before he ever made any attempt to meet with the other Apostles.

The Role of Human Confirmation

In Galatians 2:2 Paul tells us why he returned from his extended desert experience: "I went in response to a revelation and set before [the Apostles] the gospel that I preached among the Gentiles. *But I did this privately to those who seemed to be leaders, for fear that I was running or had run my race in vain.*"

Paul returned from his wilderness experience because he was seeking human confirmation for the ministry God had clearly already blessed. Paul had led many Gentiles to Christ during his wilderness experience. In one very real sense, converts like Barnabas, Timothy and Titus were confirmations of God's blessing upon Paul's ministry.

Yet there comes a time when godly leaders, who also serve by the Holy Spirit, must come to agree with God that our ministry is blessed by Him. But there is an appropriate confirmation sequence: God first confirms our ministry calling with spiritual fruit in the lives of others; it is then possible for other godly leaders to observe that fruit and affirm God's mission-call upon our lives. It is common, however, for people to get the order backwards by seeking the praise and affirmation of church leaders first.

Confirmation through Equipping

I have found that most pastors believe they are effectively "[preparing] God's people for works of service so that the body of Christ may be built up" (Eph. 4:12). In contrast, most lay people feel they are totally ill-equipped for ministry and cannot specifically cite how their pastor(s) have equipped them. Furthermore, they believe that their church lacks any intentional and consistent strategy for equipping. This may be due to

> God first confirms our ministry calling by enabling us to bear spiritual fruit in the lives of others. It is then possible for other godly leaders to observe that fruit and affirm God's mission-call upon our lives.

the fact that pastors themselves often receive very little personal equipping other than seminary coursework. It is difficult for them to extend to others something that they have never received.

I am not at all critical of seminary training—it has great value. However, the Biblical model of equipping people for ministry is vastly different from our contemporary seminary model. In the Biblical model, a rabbi calls a group of select students to follow him. And literally, the students immediately leave their vocation and family to live with the rabbi. The rabbi teaches the students, and the students watch the rabbi apply the teachings in real-life ministry situations. This involved five phases:

1. *Instruction:* The rabbi provides a Biblical foundation for ministry practice.
2. *Illustration:* The students observe the rabbi applying the teaching in a real-life ministry context.
3. *Application:* The rabbi reviews with the students what they observed, and how the Biblical teaching had been practically applied.
4. *Replication:* The students attempt to replicate the ministry practices they have observed in their rabbi.
5. *Evaluation:* The students return to report and review with the rabbi how their ministry experience has fared.

Jesus practiced this form of equipping with His disciples. Later the apostles applied this same methodology to junior leaders such as Timothy, Titus and Barnabas. Examples can be found in Mark 6, Philippians 2, Philippians 3:17 and First Timothy 3.

Most pastors today never equip their people beyond the instructional phase. Basic Bible instruction is given on Sundays, and maybe an additional weekly Bible study; but precious few church leaders develop intentional equipping strategies. In most cases people willing to serve in ministry are simply unleashed to "sink or swim" on their own. Just imagine the ministry impact that could be possible if willing Christ-followers, impassioned by the Holy Spirit, were nurtured by mature spiritual leaders who invested in them, preparing them specifically for the mission that God had called them to fulfill!

Regardless of the phase of your ministry passion—dreamer, visionary or missionary—persevere, encouraging your pastoral leaders to equip you personally for ministry. If they are not willing, then find a mature spiritual leader who will take the time to invest in you. The experience, support, counsel and accountability of mature spiritual leaders are essential elements in the success of your mission.

As you mature in your ministry, don't forget to look for "Timothys" that God brings along your path. Invest in them and equip them for ministry as you yourself desired to be equipped.

Application Summary: Create a Passion Statement

A passion statement can help you focus your life upon the dominant traits that inspire and motivate you. In many respects your passion statement will be a definition of who you are as a person. But it goes deeper than mere self-awareness; a passion statement is about your sense of mission-calling. It will bring direction and focus to your personal ministry, and it will guide your spiritual leaders to equip you more adequately for your unique ministry mission.

To write your personal passion statement, you will want to thoughtfully review the results of the assessments and worksheets you have already completed. Give consideration also to those occasions when your natural passion may have been enflamed by the Holy Spirit. Have these passions been confirmed by God or by godly people?

There is no wrong way to write a passion statement. Simply express as honestly and openly as possible your current self-perception. This is your first draft of a process that will be refined in chapter 10. It is very important that you spend considerable time in prayer as you work through this initial draft.

Review the following passion statement to help you jump-start this process.

Example:

I am passionate about creating new ministry systems and structures that empower church leaders around the world to make disciples of Christ, and to equip and mobilize those disciples for ministry service within an Internet-based global culture.

I am confident that my passion for this ministry is inspired by the Holy Spirit because it honors who God made me to be (ePesrsonality Profile: "Planner") the mission directives of Scripture (Matt. 28:18–20; Ephesians 4:11–13) and my personal sense of ministry calling.

My passion for this ministry has been confirmed through God's miraculous provision, the support of my spouse and the confirmation of ministry leaders around the world.

–David Posthuma

My Passion Statement: (*First Draft*)

A. I am passionate about:

_____

_____

_____

_____

_____

B. I am confident that my passion for this ministry is inspired by the Holy Spirit because:

_____

_____

_____

_____

_____

C. My passion for this ministry has been confirmed through:

_____

_____

_____

Chapter 5

You Are a Born Leader

A re leaders born, or are they made? The answer is both. Have you ever considered that you are a "born leader"? That's right, God created you to lead. You may not feel much like a leader at the moment, but that is probably because your mental image of what a leader looks like is skewed by a non-Biblical definition of leadership. Your mental picture of leadership probably looks something like the graphic below:

Leadership Image

What is wrong with this image of leadership? The idea that one solitary person should stand out from among the crowd, scan the horizon and lead the crowd forward into the future may sound romantic, but it is not Biblical. This image of leadership projects all the responsibility for a mission, and all the glory for accomplishing that mission, upon one person. The crowd in this graphic merely exists to follow and support the leader.

Characteristics of Biblical Leadership

In contrast, Biblically-informed leadership occurs when each Christ-follower identifies their unique functional role within the body of Christ and serves others in the context of that role. Through their ministry service, each Christ-follower positively impacts the people they serve. Jesus, the ultimate Leader, demonstrated how leaders should function when He washed His disciples' feet and commanded them to serve others in the same manner (John 13:1–17). Through this object lesson, Jesus influenced not only His disciples, but also millions upon millions of future leaders for generations to come.

This kind of leadership is clearly portrayed in *The Lord of the Rings, part 1: The Fellowship of the Ring.* I like the scene in which the dominant leaders from the various kingdoms of Third Earth come together at a secret counsel session to learn about the evil ring and the need for a leader to return the ring to the fires of Mount Doom so that it can be destroyed.

As these leaders argue with one another over the mission at hand, Frodo, a meek and gentle-spirited Hobbit, begins to yell above the fray: "I will take the ring! I will take the ring! . . . but I do not know the way."

One by one, the other leaders vow to support Frodo in his mission using their various strengths. For one, his strength is his sword. For another leader, his strength is his bow. And still for another, his strength is his ax.

If you and I had been charged with the responsibility of selecting a leader for that mission, it is unlikely that we would have selected Frodo. From outward appearances, he was not powerful or highly-skilled—but his heart was pure and he was willing to serve.

God-honoring leadership requires a humble heart-attitude. The purpose of our life mission is not to demonstrate what great leaders we are or the great works we can accomplish. Our purpose should be to lead others in a manner that demonstrates the greatness of our God and the superiority of His works. For this reason, when the prophet Samuel was given the responsibility to anoint the next king over Israel, God told him, "The Lord does not look at the things man looks at. Man looks at the outward appearance, but the Lord looks at the heart" (1 Sam. 16:6–7).

> To the extent that you or I have influence upon another person— for good or for bad— we function as a leader.

If you feel that you do not look, act or sound like a leader—good! Then your heart-attitude is likely prepared for God's purposes.

Leadership is Influence

Leadership is commonly defined as "influence." To the extent that you or I have influence upon another person—for good or for bad—we function as a leader. God intends each Christ-follower to have a significant influence upon others in this world in the context of Christ's global kingdom-mission. If this were not so, He would not have created you in the first place. You were born to lead!

Yet this influence, if it is to be truly effective, must be applied intentionally. In addition to understanding your mission, you must also identify your functional role within that mission. How I influence people will likely be different than how you influence, based upon our individual ministry temperaments. The unique manner in which each of us influences the lives of others is known as our "Leadership Style."

Your Leadership Style is closely, though not exclusively, associated with the *Relational Style* quadrant of your personality profile. If you remember, the *Relational Style* quadrant assesses how an individual relates to others on a continuum that ranges from 100 percent "Independent" (task-focused) to 100 percent "Social" (people-focused). In the majority of cases, people are not purely "Independent" or "Social"; rather they are various blends of both relational styles. The illustration on the next page breaks down this relational continuum into three categories, each consisting of two distinct Leadership Styles.

Relational Continuum

Pioneer ▶ Strategic ▶ Administrator ▶ Team Leader ▶ Pastor ▶ Encourager		
• **Visionary**	• **Motivational**	• **Relational**
• **Task Dominant**	• **Mission Tasks**	• **People Dominant**
• **Strategic**	• **Accomplishments**	• **Harmony**
• **Entreprenurial**	• **Administrative**	• **Pastoral**
Influences others by developing systems, organizations, and programs that enable other people to serve effectively.	Influences others to accomplish a mission by providing resources, organization, and motivation.	Influences others through relationships that support and encourage.

It is important, if you are to identify and effectively fulfill your God-ordained mission, that you not only understand your own leadership style but that you also understand and appreciate other leadership styles. God created all the various leadership styles and put these diversely gifted people in your life to assist you in your mission venture.

The Builder Category

People who identify with the Builder category are relational independents. They may have strong interpersonal skills, yet they think strategically and analytically. For the Builder a noble mission can only be accomplished by creating organizations, programs, systems and structures that help facilitate the goals of ministry.

The Builder category consists of two leadership profiles: *Pioneering Leader* and *Strategic Planner.* The Pioneering Leader is characterized by an *entrepreneurial* style—needing to build new organizations and programs. The Strategic Planner is characterized by an *architectural* style—needing to design the systems for new programs and ministries.

The Pioneering Leader

The Pioneering Leader is an excellent church planter and new ministry developer. The Pioneer is 100 percent motivated by a noble vision. Individuals who score as purely dominant Pioneer profiles may be viewed by some as a "flash in the pan": They light quickly, burn passionately for a short time, and then as boredom and routine settle in, they lose interest. Pioneers are creative, entrepreneurial people. They must be allowed to create new ministry organizations, programs and systems. As long as their role allows them to create, they can be satisfied for many years. However, the Pioneer should never be given ongoing administrative or interpersonal pastoral care. These responsibilities will ultimately burn-out a Pioneer.

Pioneer profiles are rare and within many churches virtually absent. This is largely due to the fact that many churches are reticent about starting new ministries and programs. The decision-makers in many church organizations tend to possess leadership styles which avoid conflict and risk; they suggest "moving slowly" whenever change is considered.

For the Pioneer who thrives on the synergy, passion and momentum of a noble vision, "moving slowly" is an exercise in frustration. As a result Pioneers often have a difficult time finding their place within established ministries. This is why so many Pioneers step outside the confines of the local church to start new church and parachurch ministries.

Pioneers often possess significant faith. They revel in "risk." They know that God can do abundantly more than we can think or ask, and they often wonder why their church and its leadership don't "think bigger" and "ask for more" from the Lord.

While Pioneers can help stir a comfortable and mission-lazy church to action, if they do not feel validated by the church leadership, they can quickly become embittered and critical. They may also be perceived as pushy, insensitive and controlling. However it is the force of their strong personalities that ultimately pulls people together to transform a vision into a mission.

The Strategic Planner

The pure Strategic Planner functions much like an architect, who designs the blueprint but does not build the building. They may effectively assist Pioneers but are not themselves entrepreneurial. Instead they are able to translate a vision into a working plan that enables others to know how they can best support a mission.

The Strategic Planner is all about planning the "details" involved in accomplishing the mission. However, they do not appreciate having to personally manage and address the details. For the Strategic Planner, the "plan" is a thing of beauty. In their mind they can envision most every step, every issue and every obstacle that will present itself if the vision is to become a ministry reality.

The Strategic Planner will become frustrated when other leaders cannot understand or value the plan. Similarly, they will become anxious when ministry leaders deviate from the plan without consulting them. The Strategic Planner views such deviations as highly dangerous, potentially jeopardizing the success of the mission—and they are probably correct in their concerns.

It is not that the Strategic Planner is trying to control everybody and everything. In reality, they can envision the consequences of an action with clarity that few other leadership types can appreciate. The plan is important to the Strategic Planner because he or she firmly believes that the plan will maximize the potential for mission success, minimize waste and ineffectiveness, and minimize harm to the ministry and to its people.

The Strategic Planner is the rarest of all leadership styles. Most ministries have no idea if they have a Strategic Planner within their congregation. Even if they do, most ministry leaders fail to utilize them effectively for one or more of the following reasons:

- Church leaders often think relationally rather than strategically and tend to devalue strategic plans.
- Many church leaders are quickly overwhelmed by the vast details of the plan devised by a Strategic Planner.
- In some cases an insecure leader may feel threatened by the Strategic Planner, fearing that he or she is "taking over" or trying to "control" the church.
- Often church leaders want to copy ministry methods that seem to succeed in other churches, rather than develop and implement an entirely new and "untested" plan.

Leadership Style Blends

While pure Pioneering Leaders and pure Strategic Planners do exist, most people in the Builder category are a blend of the two profiles. Every blend has a dominant trait. For example, my dominant trait is Pioneering Leadership. However, I also possess considerable Strategic Planner abilities. God gave me this "Builder-Blend" to enable me to begin new ministry organizations, systems, and structures, while at the same time having the insight to develop long-term strategies for project success. The graph on the next page is a report of my leadership style:

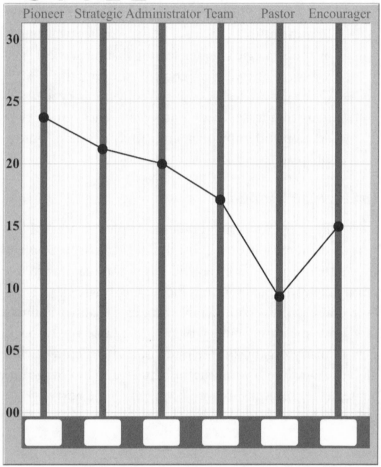

My Pioneering and Strategic scores are similar to one another. This kind of close scoring between any two adjoining style categories indicates a blended leadership style. A blend cannot exist, however, between non-adjoining categories.

For instance, a high score on both Pioneering and Pastoral is not a blend, because these two leadership styles are polar opposites. A score like that suggests a person is either confused about who he really is, or is working very hard to be something that he is not. It is common to find that pastors of local churches are confused about their leadership style. This is usually because they work so hard trying to please and appease the people around them that they lose their own identity.

When you take the Leadership Style assessment, look for a natural curve falling to the left or right of a dominant leadership style. A jagged curve within your report consisting of numerous peaks suggests internal stress and role confusion.

The Manager Category

The Manager category is characterized by a need for practical application. The Manager identifies all the real-world issues, problems and obstacles associated with any mission. Builders can get frustrated with Managers because Builders tend to feel that the synergy and momentum of the mission will carry the team through these challenges; or they may feel that their master plan is sufficient to address the issues. But Managers quickly see the many small details that a master plan cannot address. Managers hate to see "balls dropped." They become anxious when they feel the mission may be compromised because details are "falling through the cracks."

The Manager category contains two Leadership Styles: *Administrative Leader* and *Team Leader*. The Administrative Leader prefers to address the many tasks associated with the mission, while the Team Leader prefers to motivate the many people associated with the mission.

The Administrative Leader

The Administrative Leader is an ideal "detail" person. Administrators will often create "to-do" lists of all the practical tasks that must be accomplished and then work their way progressively through the lists. Most often Administrators prefer to address tasks in order of perceived priority rather than multi-task. They gain great satisfaction from checking accomplishments off their "to-do" lists.

Administrative Leaders are among the most common leadership styles found in a church or ministry. Often they serve as administrative assistants to the pastoral staff, or as deacons or treasurers. In larger ministries they may serve as a leader, or supportive leader, within a major ministry program.

The Administrator makes sure that everything is accomplished with excellence and professionalism. If they "drop the ball," which is rare, they may wrestle with shame and guilt for their failures. "Grace" is a difficult concept for Administrators to extend to themselves, although they may readily extend it to others. This is because they may at times confuse their self-worth with the tasks they must accomplish.

Administrative Leaders can struggle with several weaknesses that may obstruct the accomplishment of a mission:

1. Administrative Leaders may measure their self-perception and self-worth with their performance. If they fail to perform, they may become immobilized with guilt and shame.

2. Administrative Leaders may become overwhelmed by the many tasks at hand and seek to slow the progress of the mission to allow for more time to manage and address the many details. This is one reason why Administrators can gain a reputation as obstructionists. Fear of failure—of "dropping balls"—may cause them to try to control their environment.

    The better path for the Administrator is to learn how to delegate duties to others. However, a common response to this issue of delegation is, "If I want the job done right, I'll have to do it myself."

3. Administrative Leaders require continual affirmation from their superiors for their many positive accomplishments, particularly when they feel they have failed. Harsh and critical words of judgment or disappointment from a superior may cause them to shift into "performance overdrive." Administrators can become obsessed with trying to please superiors and atone for perceived failures, ultimately resulting in emotional and spiritual burn-out.

The Team Leader

Team Leaders are more relationally inclined than Administrative Leaders. While Administrators are consumed by tasks and details, the Team Leaders' dominant passion is to gather people around themselves and mobilize them for a mission. They understand and value the tasks associated with the mission. However, they do not want to be encumbered by the responsibility of personally accomplishing the tasks.

Team Leaders generally excel at delegating responsibilities to others. They feel an inner need to be out on the "front lines," getting their hands dirty, accomplishing real-world ministry. Nothing frustrates Team Leaders more than requiring them to sit in an office day after day, working on administrative responsibilities. Team Leaders thrive in atmospheres of "action" and typically excel at multi-tasking.

Every church needs Team Leaders. Without them church ministries would likely have many meetings but accomplish very little. The Team Leader profile is unique. Only these leaders are able to have one foot planted in the "task-oriented" world and the other foot planted in the "relationally-oriented" world. As a result, they are able to care for people and inspire them to accomplish great mission objectives.

This unique blending of care and motivation often nurtures intense feelings of loyalty between team members and the Team Leader. These feelings of loyalty can be healthy and appropriate if the Team Leader is spiritually mature, humble before God and submissive to spiritual leadership. However, these same feelings of loyalty can be used by Satan to cause considerable damage to a ministry.

The Team Leader profile is the leadership style commonly associated with a church split. In such cases, the Team Leader can point to many mission successes that have earned him or her loyalty from a significant pool of team members. Praise and admiration from team members can lead the Team Leader to become like King Nebuchadnezzar who said, "Is not this the great Babylon I have built as the royal residence, by my mighty power and for the glory of my majesty?" (Daniel 4:30). Substitute "ministry" for "Babylon" and "church" for "royal residence," and you have the attitude of the prideful Team Leader!

Prideful Team Leaders may feel they are personally responsible for the success of the church and that if only they could be unencumbered by the restrictions of their superiors, they could accomplish even greater things. Pride evolves into arrogance and leads to a profound disrespect for those in authority over the Team Leader. The scenario commonly spins off in one of three ways:

1. The prideful Team Leader is fired, and a group of his or her supporters leave the church, generating bitterness and confusion on both sides of the problem.
2. The prideful Team Leader takes over the church and supplants the senior pastor. The senior pastor leaves with a small number of loyal followers to start another church, generating bitterness and confusion on both sides of the problem.
3. The prideful Team Leader is deemed a threat to the church and its leadership and is encouraged, with the "support" of the mother church, to start a church plant across town. A significant core of the church's lay leadership leaves to start the church plant. If the issues are not addressed, competition can develop between the mother church and the church plant.

These scenarios do not need to be the ultimate path of a Team Leader. Wise church leadership will provide Team Leaders with people to whom they can be accountable—people who will help them continually check their hearts for pride. If issues of pride can be addressed when they are small, it is unlikely that significant problems will arise in the future.

Leadership Style Blends

The Team Leader/Administrator blend combines the ability to mobilize people effectively for ministry with the ability to address the administrative duties of the ministry mission. This dual role can be a recipe for ministry burnout.

People with the Team Leader/Administrator blend can for a time excel and may appear to be the ideal project leaders. However, without supportive people in their lives, those with this leadership blend can quickly become consumed with all their responsibilities. Workaholism is second nature to these individuals, and they may sacrifice their health and family in pursuit of the mission and its many tasks.

The Nurturer Category

The Nurturer category is highly focused on relationships. Those who identify with this category consider it their mission to socially interact with people and, through those relationships, to serve them. They tend to devalue ministry organizations and programs. In fact, it is not uncommon for them to feel that man-made structures and systems actually get in the way of ministry. They often wonder why other people cannot minister as they do—personally serving people's needs directly. The Nurturer category is characterized by people who are likable, tender-hearted, sensitive, compassionate and good listeners.

The Nurturer category consists of two leadership styles: *Pastoral* and *Encouraging*. While both leadership types are highly relational, the Pastoral Leader's preoccupation is, "How are WE doing?" while the Encouraging Leader's preoccupation is, "How are YOU doing?"

The Pastoral Leader

Pastoral Leaders are generally very likable and amiable people. Their nature puts people at ease and helps them feel that at the moment, they are the most important person in the Pastor's life. This is a very attractive quality.

Pastors are naturally concerned about the welfare of the group, whether the congregation as a whole or a particular ministry team. This does not mean that they have no concern for individuals, for they care deeply. However, Pastors appreciate the fact that people exist as the "body of Christ." Pastors seek the health of the body and so value and nurture interpersonal harmony and cooperation.

Pastors generally dislike administrative duties. For Pastors, "being in Christ" is far more important than "doing for Christ." They need to get out of the office and into people's lives. If they are not permitted significant periods of interpersonal interaction, they may become discouraged and depressed.

Pastors do not effectively cast vision or create strategic plans. At best, they may seek out a successful ministry paradigm in use by other ministries and attempt to transplant that program within their church context. Vision-casting and strategic planning are task-oriented skills that God never instilled within pastors.

It grieves my heart when a high-powered church board of community and business leaders demands that their pastor cast vision and create strategic plans for the entire ministry. God never designed pastors for such tasks, and it is inappropriate for church boards to expect people with the Pastor profile to meet these unrealistic demands.

Pastors excel at visitation, encouragement, mentorship, spiritual nurture, small group shepherding and counseling. They may also possess limited preaching and teaching abilities. Their instructional style will convey a greater passion for the people they serve than for the content itself—in short, most pastors are not dynamic Biblical expositors. They will tend to apply Biblical truth as a guide to encourage people to love and care for one another.

Pastors value relational and spiritual harmony so highly that they may overlook discord and division, in the hope that the problems will work themselves out. Pastors tend to avoid conflict and risk. When a problem arises within the congregation, or a change in the ministry is needed, they may be slow to address it. When a new ministry venture is suggested, they will look for proven models to implement. Their overriding concern is that people be protected from harm, yet sometimes when a bandage is pulled off too slowly, it only prolongs the suffering. This is a difficult lesson for many pastors to learn.

Pastors should be responsible for the spiritual welfare of the team or congregation. However, they should not have oversight of the various task-intensive functions and ministries within the church. These duties are best served by Team Leaders or Administrators.

When Pastors are placed in positions of responsibility over mission teams, the teams will likely have many meetings and accomplish very little. Pastors tend to "drop balls" that others have to pick up. For this reason, pastors require the assistance of Administrators to help ensure that the details and tasks associated with their ministry responsibilities are accomplished.

Leadership Style Blends

A blend between Team Leader and Pastoral Leader is entirely possible. Within a church context, this blended leadership style may indeed be the ideal senior pastor. This profile balances the need for mission with the need to care for the spiritual and emotional needs of the people who help accomplish the mission. Vision casting, strategic planning and administration will never be skills exhibited by the Team Leader/Pastor blend. However, if those with these skills are included in the leadership core, the ministry will likely strike a healthy balance between mission and compassion.

The Encouraging Leader

Encouraging Leaders are generally likable yet quiet and introspective people. Their nature is similar to the Pastor in that they seek to put people at ease and desire to help them feel that at the moment, they are the most important person in the Encourager's life. Encouragers often play the role of counselor or mentor as they relate to and serve others. Encouragers are not at all task-oriented and may distance themselves from serving within the local church programming. Encouragers tend to devalue programs and would rather be involved with people directly through interpersonal relationships.

In one respect there exists a parallel trait between Pioneers and Encouragers. Pioneers seek to analyze systems and structures for ministry, whereas Encouragers often seek to analyze people in order to minister to them more effectively.

In a discipleship context, Encouragers generally excel as one-on-one personal mentors. They may also enjoy a counseling ministry, dealing with issues such as abuse, marriage and child rearing. They often serve effectively within recovery ministries that address issues of addiction and spiritual bondage.

Encouragers firmly believe that "Each of you should look not only to your own interests, but also to the interests of others" (Phil. 2:4). They resonate with Paul's command to "Carry each other's burdens, and in this way you will fulfill the law of Christ" (Gal. 6:2).

One challenge Encouragers struggle with, however, is that they may inappropriately take upon themselves the burdens that other people bear. It is possible for Encouragers to care so deeply about the people they minister to, and desire so intensely to "fix" their problems, that they begin to have difficulty disassociating themselves from the problems of others. When Encouragers begin to demonstrate anxiety or undue worry over the decisions of other people, they may be progressing down an unhealthy path that could ultimately result in excessive stress and eventual ministry burnout.

Encouragers should never assume leadership over teams or programs. Such task-oriented leadership roles are not in the core make-up of Encouragers. They resist administrative duties. For Encouragers, the mission is meeting with and helping people directly; any other task-oriented obligations will be likely viewed as a serious distraction from their mission focus.

Leadership Style Blends

It is entirely possible to be a blend of the Pastoral Leader and Encouraging Leader profiles. In such cases the leader will likely exhibit a passion for the welfare of the group, as well as taking a personal interest in the welfare of each individual in the group. This blended leadership style is best suited for small groups of people requiring ongoing pastoral care.

The Pioneer/Team Leader Blend

There is one unique leadership style blend that is not comprised of adjoining styles: the Team Leader/Pioneer blend. This blend consists of a dominant Team Leader style score and a secondary Pioneer style score. However, this is not a natural blend.

This blend may occur when Team Leaders have an opportunity to serve alongside Pioneers, supporting them in an entrepreneurial venture. In these situations Team Leaders learn that they share a key value with Pioneers—the primacy of "mission." This shared value may inspire Team Leaders to identify closely with Pioneers and to respect their leadership abilities.

However, Team Leaders are dissimilar to Pioneers in that they do not typically have the vision or the independence to begin an entrepreneurial venture on their own. Team Leaders prefer to assemble and mobilize teams of people for the accomplishment of a mission. For this reason, on the rare occasion that they take the lead in an entrepreneurial venture, they will require a network of encouraging people to support them.

The Flat-Line Leadership Style

A Flat-Line Leadership Style is one in which no leadership style clearly dominates; all styles score approximately +/ -5 points from each other. Individuals who receive Flat-Line reports typically meet one of two conditions: Either they do not know themselves very well, or more commonly, they are seeking to conform to the perceived expectations of others around them. The habitual repetition of this conformist behavior can lead to confusion regarding their true leadership identity.

This identity crisis often occurs with people who have served in ministry for extensive periods. The unique interpersonal demands associated with ministry may influence them to repress their natural leadership style in an effort to "please and appease" the demands and expectations of the people they serve. However, no person was ever designed by God to be "all things to all people."

The Flat-Line profile represents an unfortunate and painful state and indicates internal anxiety and a deep desire for acceptance. Only through a personal interview process, and possibly counseling, can people caught in a "please and appease" lifestyle re-discover who God truly intended them to be. It is crucial that they gain freedom in Christ so that they can serve their Lord according to their true created order.

Leadership Style Overview

Now that you have been introduced to the various dynamics associated with leadership styles, it is time to discover your personal Leadership Style. Complete the Leadership Style Worksheet (on next page); it will help you in developing your life mission plan (Chapter 10).

Part 1: Summarize Your Leadership Style

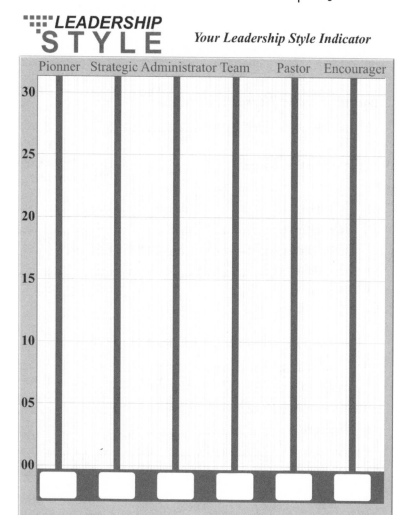

Instructions:

1. Go to www.assessme.org and complete the Leadership Style Assessment©.

2. Print your assessment report from the website or refer to

your Leadership Style report in Appendix C. (Note: The appendix includes all six Leadership Style reports.)
3. Plot your scores on the chart on previous page.
4. Record your answers to the worksheet questions below.

Leadership Style Worksheet

A. My primary Leadership Style is: _____

B. I can affirm that my dominant Leadership Style strengths include:
   • Strength #1 _____
   • Strength #2 _____
   • Strength #3 _____
C. I can affirm that my Leadership Style weaknesses include:
   • Weakness #1 _____
   • Weakness #2 _____
   • Weakness #3 _____

Part 2: Validate Your Leadership Style

D. Please identify specific examples in your past where you have applied your Leadership Style within the context of ministry (If not ministry, please identify the context).
   • Example #1 _____
   • Example #2 _____
   • Example #3 _____

E. After reflection, on the occasions in which you have served according to your Leadership Style, how did you feel about yourself in relationship to your service role? (e.g., satisfied, fulfilled, motivated, at peace)

_____

_____

_____

Chapter 6

Building Three-Strand Cord Leadership Teams

What happens in your church when a key program leader moves on? Does the program appear to disintegrate? Does your church leadership scramble to uphold the program as it exists? Do committee members squabble among themselves about how to keep the program running?

Most church leadership structures are based upon either a "Point Person" model or a "Committee" model. Both of these models present serious organizational and leadership flaws that can be devastating to the long-term effectiveness of a ministry.

The Point Person Model

In the Point Person leadership model, based upon a top-down paradigm, church leaders seek to identify one person to be responsible for a ministry. Once that person is identified, a second layer of ministry supporters are recruited. Ths illustration below provides a graphical depiction of this model.

Point Person Model

The Point Person leadership model is prone to problems with *Burnout, Accountability* and *Succession Planning.*

POINT PERSON

SUPPORT STAFF

Burnout occurs when one person is expected to recruit, train, lead, motivate and manage the team, address the many administrative duties associated with the team, and support the spiritual and emotional needs of the team. This is an impossible task!

The Point Person leadership model expects one person to be all things to all people, rather than respecting their God-ordained leadership styles and personality dynamics. This model is fundamentally unloving and unhealthy, sacrificing the emotional and spiritual welfare of ministry staff and lay leaders, and setting them up for eventual burnout.

When they leave their positions in utter exhaustion, these abused leaders often feel like they are letting the church down and letting God down. They are generally unwilling to reinvest their lives in ministry mission until they have received significant healing. In many cases, they never return to ministry.

Lack of Accountability often occurs because the top-down structure means the support staff lack the necessary authority to hold the Point Person accountable. Peers and superiors of the Point Person are generally so consumed with their own ministry responsibilities that they do not provide accountability until a problem becomes obviously apparent. By that time, the situation is often out of control.

> The Point Person leadership model is fundamentally unloving and unhealthy, sacrificing the emotional and spiritual welfare of ministry staff and lay leaders, and setting them up for burnout.

When leaders are not held accountable for their actions—or lack of action—they may fall victim to unsound doctrine, temptation, pride, arrogance, control issues, laziness and numerous other negative leadership flaws that can have devastating consequences for a ministry.

One church I worked with is a perfect example of the problems associated with a lack of accountability among Point People. The entire church was built upon the ministry service of the senior pastor and the associate pastor. The church was surprised and directionless when the senior pastor, without warning, resigned and moved his family to a different state, all in the course of one week. Furthermore, the associate pastor declined to help lead the church during this difficult time.

The associate pastor had originally been hired to serve a dual role of youth and worship. However he had convinced the church board that this dual role was too demanding, and he had been allowed to continue his full-time position (with benefits) focusing exclusively upon leading the worship ministry. It soon became clear, however, that the associate pastor was selecting songs thirty minutes before the service, not holding practices and not developing additional musicians and singers. At most he was serving twelve to fifteen hours per week, while being paid to serve the church full-time.

A lack of accountability in the church allowed the associate pastor to perform his duties poorly, and made it possible for the senior pastor to abandon his "flock" without warning or preparation.

Lack of Succession Planning is evident when the single person in charge of a ministry suddenly leaves, and all of the knowledge and expertise leaves with them. Most churches lack a strategy for leadership transition, particularly if the leadership paradigm utilizes the Point Person model. Under this model, it may take the church many months to identify and recruit a new leader, and many more months for that new leader to rebuild the ministry program. Then if this point person burns out—or maybe I should say *when* this point person burns out—the dysfunctional cycle is repeated again.

The lack of Succession Planning affects every level of a ministry organization. This is blatantly illustrated by the many phone calls I receive from churches whose webmaster (the person who develops and manages the church website) has suddenly resigned and taken all the development files, graphics, code and access passwords. As a result the church has no option but to rebuild the website from scratch. Organizations lacking a succession strategy waste human and financial resources, reducing the overall effectiveness of the ministry.

The Committee Model

The Committee Model seeks to avoid the pitfalls of the Point Person model by providing an oligarchic (committee-based) leadership structure. Committees are often comprised of people who share a common interest in a particular ministry program and who are "willing" to serve, and make decisions based upon majority rule.

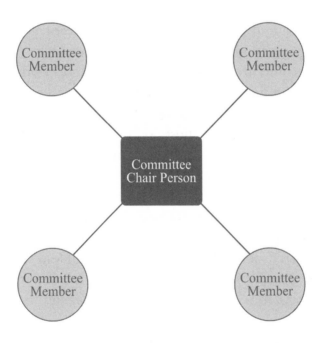

Committee Model

In most oligarchic leadership structures, there is not a clear line of authority or responsibility for each member of the committee. Committee paradigms generally suffer from *Role Confusion* and *Role Competition*.

Role Confusion occurs when responsibilities are assigned to committee members arbitrarily based upon the various tasks that must be accomplished and have little to do with the divinely ordained mission for each person's life. Because each person's "area of responsibility" is limited to various assigned tasks, the committee members tend to struggle with a limited sense of personal ownership and do not generally make a long-term emotional investment in the ministry.

In the end the committee paradigm generally suffers from unfocused leadership, resulting in many meetings, but few ministry accomplishments. Committee members typically feel the committee simply assigns them more "work" to accomplish in their already busy lives.

Role Competition is also very common within the Committee model. Because most committees are comprised of volunteers who share a common ministry interest, several committee members may have the same or similar leadership styles. For example, a committee responsible for starting a new ministry may include three Pioneering Leaders who will probably squabble over competing visions of how the ministry should develop and who should lead the development process. In-fighting is an extremely common problem associated with committee-based leadership.

The Three-Strand-Cord Model

You and I are called by God to serve Him in the context of a team, as members of the body of Christ. Your ministry mission will require that you learn how to work with people who are very different from you. You must not only learn to work with them but also to trust and rely on them.

Ecclesiastes 4:12 tells us that "A cord of three strands is not easily broken." The three-strand cord in this passage is a metaphor for interpersonal commitment and cooperation, with the number three signifying completeness. I believe that a healthy, "complete" leadership team consists of individuals who function in three very important roles: *Administrator*, *Team Leader* and *Nurturing Leader (i.e., Pastoral or Encouraging)*. I refer to the combination of these functional roles as the *Three-Strand-Cord Leadership* model.

Three-Strand-Cord Leadership

Three-Strand-Cord
Leadership Model

Administrator

Team Leader

Nurturer

The Three-Strand-Cord Leadership model requires the intentional identification and empowerment of individuals to fulfill three functional roles: Administrator, Team Leader and Nurturer. These functional roles are not arbitrary job descriptions but functional roles based on assessed leadership styles.

Each functional role (Administrator, Team Leader, and Nurturer) represents a God-ordained and God-designed style of leadership. As such, each person is able to focus upon their specific area of expertise. The Administrator is naturally passionate about addressing the ministry details. The Team Leader is naturally passionate about gathering people together and motivating them to accomplish a great mission for the Kingdom of Christ. The Nurturing Leader naturally desires to care for the emotional and spiritual welfare of the ministry team as well as for the people to whom the team ministers.

The Three-Strand-Cord leadership model does not require your ministry to triple your current staff. Rather, the model suggests that co-leaders be recruited (in many cases these will be lay leaders) to complement the Leadership Style of each person overseeing areas of ministry within the organ-ization. For example, if the Student Ministries Director displays a Team Leader style of influence, then the Director would likely benefit from the assistance of an Administrator and a Nurturer.

> The Three-Strand-Cord leadership model does not require your ministry to triple your current staff; lay co-leaders can be recruited.

Three-Strand-Cord Leadership Model

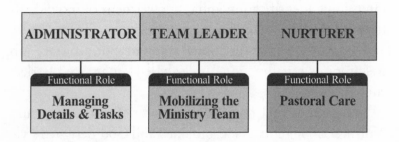

ADMINISTRATOR	TEAM LEADER	NURTURER
Functional Role	Functional Role	Functional Role
Managing Details & Tasks	Mobilizing the Ministry Team	Pastoral Care

The following crucial dynamics of this model address the problem issues commonly experienced by the Committee and Point Person leadership models:

1. Defined Functional Roles
2. Accountable Authority
3. Succession Planning

Defined Functional Roles

The Three-Strand-Cord Leadership model, by its very nature, does not permit *Role Confusion* or *Role Competition*. While each member of the leadership team will readily acknowledge the value that their fellow teammates bring to the team, the God-designed natures of each team member do not want to be encumbered with the responsibilities provided by their teammates.

Administrators have no desire to be involved in the highly-relational responsibilities of the Team Leader or Nurturing Leader. Team Leaders naturally dislike intrusions into their lives, such as administrative tasks and pastoral care, that would keep them from moving the ministry team forward to accomplish the mission.

> Under no conditions should one person "wear two hats." Team-based leadership works best when every person serves from their dominant leadership style.

The heart of the nurturing Leader is focused on caring for people and becomes frustrated when interpersonal ministry is impeded by administrative duties and mission objectives.

If people with leadership style blends are positioned cooperatively within a leadership team, it is unlikely that *Role Competition* will become an issue. An individual possessing a Team Leader/Administrative Leader blend will still be a dominant Team Leader, and will naturally prefer to serve from his or her dominant area of expertise. The fact that this person also possesses sub-dominant abilities as an Administrator will likely result in an ability to communicate and empathize effectively with the needs of the Administrator. Under no conditions should one person "wear two hats." Team-based leadership works best when every person serves from their dominant leadership style.

Authority with Accountability

The Three-Strand-Cord leadership model provides a built-in accountability structure. The importance of providing leadership accountability became apparent to me when I was fresh out of seminary. I began working with a group of people to plant a church. The Lord provided a building for only $250 a month, and our small congregation began renovations. Because our budget was limited, we asked for and received many donations from both people and companies. One of these donations was a door, which soon became known as the "devil-in-the-door."

Our workers stained the door and hung it in one of the back rooms. Later a relative of one of the elders (who had a vivid imagination) commented that the wood grain of the door kind of looked like a demon. In no time at all, this elder and his family had many of our immature new believers in an uproar over the "devil-in-the-door." People began taking pictures of the door and even used video cameras to see if the "devil" image would move.

As ridiculous as this situation may sound, it was a serious crisis of faith for many of our people at the time. Some had become so enflamed by this issue that they insisted that the door be removed and burned. We painted the door so that the grain pattern was no longer visible. I then spent several weeks publicly and privately trying to reason from Scripture that what people had seen in horror films was not true Christ-centered spirituality. Still, in the middle of the night, someone with a key to the church stole the door, and it was never seen again.

The "devil-in-the-door" scenario occurred because I had not yet learned how to properly hold people accountable and how to build team-based ministries with interpersonal accountability structures. Many months later the same elder, who had inspired fear, anxiety, division and distrust by inciting the "devil-in-the-door" situation used these same strategies to cause a church split. While the elder's entire family had sinned against God and our young congregation through their divisive behaviors, I also had sinned against God and our young congregation by failing to establish accountability structures that would protect the church from harm.

How many church splits and unplanned "church plants" have occurred as a direct result of poor accountability? While the Three-Strand-Cord leadership model cannot guarantee that your ministry will never experience leadership problems, it does provide the necessary accountability structure to reduce the potential damage that unhealthy leaders might otherwise inflict upon Christ's church.

The Three-Strand-Cord leadership model provides built-in accountability because the functional roles represent intersecting areas of ministry responsibility. Administrators naturally feel an obligation to address all the details related to the ministry with excellence and professionalism. Team

Leaders naturally feel responsible to mobilize people for ministry and do not want anything to obstruct the mission. Nurturers naturally feel responsible for the spiritual and emotional welfare of the team and the people impacted by the team. If any one leadership team member were to become functionally unhealthy, that ill-health would have a direct impact upon the ministries of the other two leadership team members.

The Three-Strand-Cord leadership model holds team members responsible for correcting, exhorting and restoring one another in Christ (see Matt. 18:15–16, 2 Cor. 13:1, 1 Tim. 5:19, Gal. 6:1, Titus 3:10). If a leadership team member refuses to listen to the correction of their teammates, Scripture states that they should bring the matter before church leadership. If the inappropriate behaviors continue after that, the leader must be removed and replaced. The remaining team members will provide the continuity needed to ensure that the overall ministry does not suffer.

Succession Planning

How we leave a ministry is just as important as how we come into a ministry. *Succession planning* is the intentional recruitment and training of the person(s) who will inherit our ministry position and propel our ministry legacy. We all desire to invest our lives into a Christ-centered mission that will last. But, without intentional systems in place that ensure healthy succession planning, ministries will inevitably experience leadership "holes," resulting in the deterioration of the ministry's impact.

> We all desire to invest our lives into a Christ-centered mission that will last.

The Three-Strand-Cord leadership model utilizes Succession Planning at two distinct levels. "Cross-category" succession planning involves transitioning a new ministry project, once established, into a stable ministry program. "Category-specific" succession planning involves the intentional identification and development of future leaders within each of the six leadership style categories: Pioneer, Strategic Planner, Administrator, Team Leader, Pastor and Encourager.

Cross-Category Succession Planning

"Cross-category" succession planning involves transitioning the responsibilities of a ministry project initiated by *Builders* into the hands of *Managers*, who are better equipped to ensure the success of the mission over an extended period of time. The drive, independence and strategic abilities of the Builder were the exact qualities required to initiate the ministry mission. Yet once the ministry stabilizes, it becomes crucial that more people be involved to make the mission a success. Managers are ideally suited to recruit and supervise a larger ministry team. They are more likely to commit to the ministry mission for an extensive period of time, whereas Builders can quickly become bored and begin to look forward to their next building projects.

Cross-Category Succession Planning

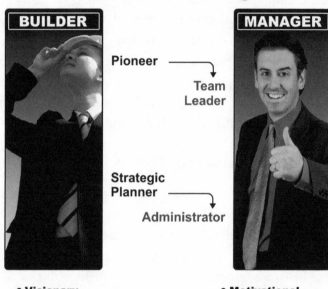

| **BUILDER** | | **MANAGER** |

Pioneer ⟶ Team Leader

Strategic Planner ⟶ Administrator

• Visionary

• Task Dominant

• Strategic

• Entreprenurial

Influences others by developing systems, organizations, and programs that enable other people to serve effectively.

• Motivational

• Mission Tasks

• Accomplishments

• Administrative

Influences others to accomplish a mission by providing resources, organization, and motivation.

Pioneer to Team Leader

It is important to note that in a new ministry venture, initially led by a Pioneering Leader, the Pioneer's role and responsibilities should eventually acquiesce to a Team Leader. Church leadership should take care to be open and honest about the succession plan. The Pioneer should participate in the training of the Team Leader, and the Team Leader should be respectful of the Pioneer. The Pioneer should be able to publicly affirm and transfer leadership authority of the ministry to the Team Leader.

Emotionally, Pioneers may feel like they have birthed a baby, and now are handing the baby over to adoptive parents and walking away. Healthy succession planning therefore necessitates that ministry leadership help Pioneer Leaders identify their next ministry start-up venture before relieving them of their current responsibilities.

Strategic Planner to Administrator

In a new ministry venture, the Strategic Planner role and responsibilities generally acquiesce to an Administrative Leader. While the Strategic Planner is the architect of the ministry plan, the Administrator can effectively interpret the strategic plan and help keep the entire ministry team on track. However, when an individual possesses a clear Strategic Planner/Administrator leadership style blend, it is possible that the succession plan will merely involve a redefining of role responsibilities.

Category-Specific Succession Planning

The illustration below shows how Category-Specific Succession Planning can be accomplished within the context of a Three-Strand-Cord leadership team. This same principle should also be applied with Pioneers and Strategic Planners.

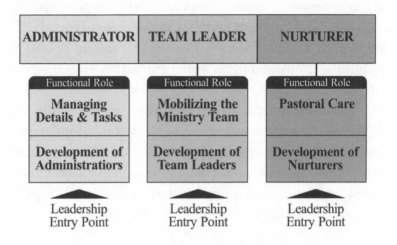

The Three-Strand-Cord leadership model provides several leadership entry points. The goal is to create a culture in which proven leaders of each leadership style (Pioneer, Strategic, Administrative, Team Leader, Pastor and Encourager) mentor developing leaders who possess the same leadership style.

Remember the principle of "mission myopia"? People naturally gather around them others who are similar to themselves. We can use this principle in a positive manner to encourage six leadership development tracks that provide resource pools for team member succession. Developing leaders learn and practice their leadership abilities under the care and supervision of successful leaders possessing the same leadership style. While they learn and prove themselves faithful, the developing leaders may provide support for their mentors by assisting them in various tasks. When the day does come for a member of a leadership team to step down, the leadership team will have a pool of trained leaders within each leadership style category with proven capability.

Many churches may already use a bench-mark example of this leadership development and succession planning strategy within their small group ministry programs. The strategy encourages small group leaders to mentor a member within the group, and when the small group has grown, and the developing leader has matured, the small group splits, giving birth to a new small group—and the process of replication begins anew.

This strategy can be effective within a small group context because by its nature small groups are led by Nurturing Leaders. These Nurturing Leaders identify people within the group who are much like themselves and begin to mentor them for future leadership positions.

Where this model breaks down, however, is with people who possess differing leadership styles. Ministry organizations applying the small group replication model have identified a successful leadership development program for one-third of the potential leadership pool: the Nurturing Leaders. Meanwhile, two-thirds of the potential leaders, comprised of Builders and Managers, must fend for themselves.

In fact in many of our churches today, there is so much emphasis on relationally-based cell ministry that Builders and Managers often feel like limbs of the body that have been programmatically severed. The church programs and job descriptions simply do not fit their leadership styles. The challenge for ministry leaders is to include Builders and Managers in defined leadership roles and to stimulate leadership training, replication and planned succession at every level.

Assembling the Leadership Team

The Leadership Style Assessment is designed specifically to help individuals not only understand their personal leadership style but also understand how they fit within a leadership team. Armed with this knowledge, leaders are able to build healthy and effective leadership teams for any ministry based on the Three-Strand-Cord model. Let's see how this works using actual assessment results from the Leadership Style Assessment tool.

Building the Team – Administrator

This Leadership Style graph on the next page represents an Administrative leader and possibly a leadership blend between Strategic Planner and Administrator. This particular leadership blend suggests that this individual would be very capable of translating a vision into its many tasks and would ensure that the tasks were accomplished appropriately and in a timely manner. But while this person is naturally skilled by God to address the many tasks of the mission, they are less suited for assembling and motivating a team to accomplish the ministry mission and even less suited to provide for the emotional and spiritual care of the team. Therefore we will want to identify ministry partners who will complement this Administrator.

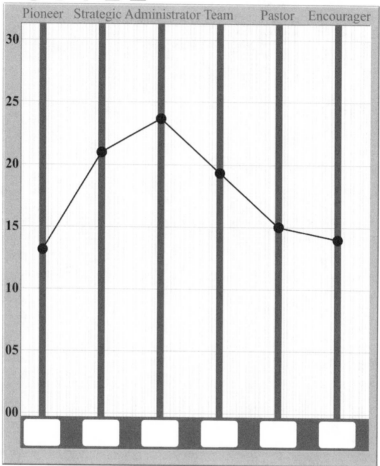

Let's now identify a Team Leader to come alongside our Administrator and help recruit, mobilize, equip and motivate the ministry team. When the reports of these leadership-types are overlaid, they may appear as displayed in the illustration on the next page.

Building the Team – Administrator/Team Leader

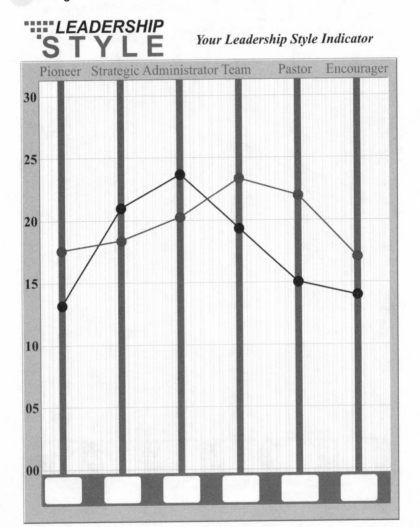

At this point I should make one clarification regarding the scoring process. Different people will score themselves more liberally or more conservatively. DO NOT interpret the point-scale as a measure of how effective a person will be in any leadership position. The point scale merely reflects an individual's self-perception; it is not an indication of whether he or she will be a competent and successful leader.

The point scale is relative to each individual only—how they measure against themselves—and is not relative to how another person has scored. For example, the Team Leader in our graphic scored approximately twenty-two points on the scale. Another Team Leader may score only fifteen points on the scale. Both may be effective Team Leaders; the differences in score-levels reflect how critically they judge themselves. In summary, higher scores typically reflect a less self-abasing person, while lower scores typically reflect a more self-critical person.

Now our leadership team consists of an Administrative Leader to address the many details and tasks associated with the ministry mission and a Team Leader to recruit, mobilize, equip and motivate the ministry team. It still does not have, however, a dedicated leader to oversee the emotional and spiritual welfare of the ministry team. So let's recruit a Pastoral Leader who is team-oriented (compared to an Encouraging Leader who is individually-oriented) and add that person to our leadership team. The overlapping Leadership Styles may look like the graph in the illustration on the next page.

Building the Team – Administrator/Team Leader/Pastor

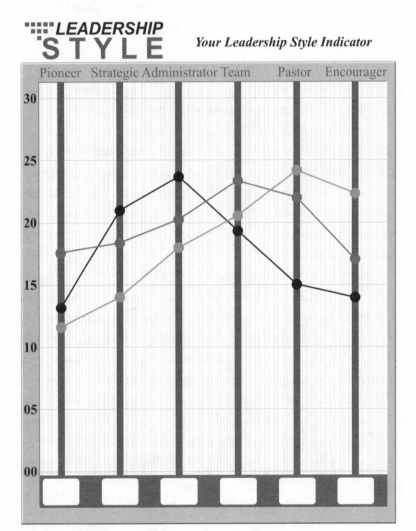

We now have a Three-Strand-Cord leadership team comprised of people who are serving according to their divinely-designed leadership styles. Each person has clearly defined functional roles and responsibilities within the team, so there is very little chance of *role confusion* or *role competition* occurring. Positioning people to serve from their strengths allows them to focus their energy in areas where they will most likely succeed and be least likely to experience stress and fatigue. The cooperation among the leadership team illustrates the importance of the entire body of Christ and that its members need one another to effectively accomplish their part in the Great Co-Mission.

> *When we serve according to our created leadership style, we function as living illustrations of the various ministry roles addressed by each member of the Godhead.*

The Trinitarian Model

The Three-Strand-Cord Leadership model also illustrates a second important theological picture; it is a human depiction of the divine Trinity: Father, Son and Holy Spirit. When we serve according to our created leadership style, we function as living illustrations of the various ministry roles addressed by each member of the Godhead.

Trinitarian Model

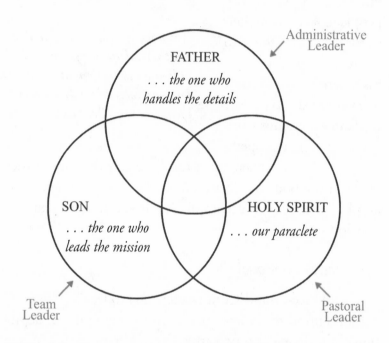

Heavenly Father, Our Administrative Leader

God the Father functions as our Creator (Strategic Planner) and Administrator. God is the architect of all of creation, and through His wisdom administers His creation. We pray to Him for all the details and needs in our lives. Jesus instructs us in the Lord's Prayer (Matt. 6:9) to direct our petitions to God the Father. Our Heavenly Father will provide for His children in a manner that is always for our good and for the accomplishment of the mission for which He created us.

One of God's names found in the Old Testament is *Jehovah Jireh*, which means "God our provider." Similarly, human Administrators function as resource providers, addressing the many details and needs associated with any ministry mission.

Jesus Christ, Our Team Leader

Jesus Christ is the ultimate Team Leader. It is Christ who established the Great Co-Mission when He ordered His followers to "go and make disciples of all nations, baptizing them in the name of the Father and of the Son and of the Holy Spirit, and teaching them to obey everything I have commanded you. And surely I will be with you always, to the very end of the age" (Matthew 28:19–20).

Jesus actively participates in the Great Co-Mission even now through the lives of each and every faithful Christ-follower. Christ promised us that He would build His church, and the gates of hell would not stand against it (Matthew 16:18).

When people who have been designed by God to influence this world through the Team Leader profile attract and motivate others for ministry mission, they are simply reflecting the Team Leader nature of Jesus Christ. This identification with Christ's ministry mission is also true of the Pioneer profile, in that the Pioneer shares with the Team Leader a common passion for mission.

Holy Spirit, Our Pastoral Leader

The Holy Spirit functions as our Pastoral Leader. One of the descriptive names given to the Holy Spirit is *Paraclete*.

This Greek word means to "come alongside" or "support." When people with the Pastor and Encourager leadership styles serve others through interpersonal ministry, they become human expressions of the primary ministry role of the Holy Spirit. These godly men and women function as *paracletes*, skilled at "coming alongside others" to support their emotional and spiritual development.

I cannot imagine a better illustration of the Triune Godhead than when Christ's church functions, at every level within its local ministry structure, according to the Three-Strand-Cord leadership model. I believe it is crucial that each Christ-follower identifies his or her leadership style in relation to the functional roles of the Trinity, since only the Godhead can provide us with perfect ministry role models. Without this identification, our role models consist of imperfect human beings who can only serve imperfectly.

Leadership Style Worksheet

Let's now review your personal Leadership Style. Review the summary results from chapter five, and expand upon those results in the form below.

A. My primary Leadership Style is: _____

B. If I am to maximize the success of my ministry mission, I should seek to partner with other ministry leaders who complement my Leadership Style. My ministry partners should include:
- A _____ Leader
- A _____ Leader

C. Succession Planning:

    1. Do I currently have a mentor who is equipping me to grow in ministry effectiveness?

      • If Yes, list name: _____

      • If No, identify potential mentors who share your leadership style: _____

    2. Am I currently mentoring and equipping others with similar leadership styles to my own, helping them to grow in ministry effectiveness?

      • If Yes, list name(s): _____

      • If No, identify potential candidates who share your leadership style: _____

D. My leadership style most closely emulates which member of the Trinity?

    • _____ My Heavenly Father, to whom I address my ministry needs

    • _____ My Savior and mission team leader

    • _____ My Paraclete, who directly ministers to me and supports my life and ministry

Chapter 7

You Are
Gifted for Ministry

As you begin this chapter, I am sure that one question has crossed your mind: Why did I wait until now to discuss spiritual gifts, when spiritual gift assessments are probably the tool most commonly used by churches?

The reason is simple: We cannot begin to understand the proper use of spiritual gifts God has given to us until we first come to appreciate our God-ordained personalities and leadership styles.

Our God-given spiritual gifts will always be filtered through our God-given personalities. For example, let's imagine that two people took a spiritual gift assessment and that they both received high scores for the gift of leadership. However, the two candidates possess very different personality profiles. The first candidate is highly relational and so would likely excel at leading a small group of people. In contrast, the second candidate is highly visionary and would likely excel in leading teams of people to plant new churches.

If we failed to consider the unique ministry temperaments of our two candidates, placing the relational leader in charge of a church plant and the visionary leader in charge of a small group, the result would likely be frustration, and ultimately, ministry failure. Our ministry temperament always determines how we apply the practical ministry gifts God has chosen to develop in our lives.

> You and I cannot begin to understand how to properly use whatever spiritual gifts God may have bestowed upon us until we first come to appreciate our God-ordained personalities and leadership styles.

The spiritual gift assessment used by AssessMe.org and E-Church Essentials allows each person to identify how their dominant giftedness is best expressed in their life and ministry. The various gift "expressions" take into account personality dynamics, along with other skills.

What are Spiritual Gifts?

The spiritual gift assessment used in this book is entitled "GraceGifts" because this is the literal Greek name for spiritual gifts in the New Testament. To help us fully appreciate spiritual giftedness, let's explore a word-play that is only perceptible in the Greek language of the New Testament. The illustration on the next page depicts three interrelated Greek words which lay a foundation for a proper understanding of spiritual giftedness.

The underlying concept behind spiritual gifts begins with the root word *chara*, which may be translated as "joy." God desires that you and I experience joy, not only as we use the gifts He gives us and see God working through us, but also because of the spiritual fruit we bear when we are faithful to our divine mission.

The next variation of the root word *chara* (joy) is the Greek word *charis* (grace). *Charis* means that you and I get all of Christ's benefits, solely at Christ's expense. There is nothing you and I can do to earn the benefits offered to us in Christ Jesus. Grace is rooted in joy because God's grace, manifested in many forms, is given to us as a gift.

One form of grace relevant to our discussion is *charismata*, literally translated "grace gifts." *Charismata* are most commonly understood as "spiritual gifts" within the context of the church. These "grace gifts" are special enablements, granted by the Holy Spirit, that allow us to accomplish our divine mission in the context of Christ's Great Co-Mission.

There is nothing you and I can do to earn these gifts. They are bestowed freely upon us through the wisdom and foreknowledge of our Lord and Savior Jesus Christ, by the power of the Holy Spirit. In First Corinthians 12:11, Paul tells us that the Holy Spirit "gives [gifts] to each [person], just as he determines." Our Lord knows our mission well.

He made us ideally suited to accomplish our mission. For this reason, He will bestow the exact gifts we need so that we can complete His mission successfully.

The Apostle Paul tells us, "Now about spiritual gifts, brothers, I do not want you to be ignorant" (1 Cor. 12:1). And yet it seems many people do indeed remain confused and misinformed about how to identify and mobilize true spiritual giftedness effectively. This confusion stems in part from uncertainty experienced by many Christ-followers as to whether they possess the Holy Spirit; they may also question the role of the Holy Spirit within their lives.

This is why Paul goes on to explain, "Now to each one the manifestation of the Spirit is given for the common good" (12:7). Every Christ-follower can be assured that he or she does indeed have at least one spiritual gift. When the Greek word translated "manifestation" is applied to a person, it means to "make oneself known." One way we can know that the Holy Spirit has "made Himself known" in our lives is through the evidence of spiritual gifts bestowed upon us.

Types of Giftedness

God manifests the gifts of the Holy Spirit either through *augmentation* of the natural gifts He has already designed within our DNA, or through *revelation*, for use in the moment.

Augmentation of Natural Giftedness

The practical ministry gifts are generally augmentations (i.e., amplifications) of skills that have been developing since birth. You will recall from our earlier discussion that our practical ministry gifts are always influenced by our ministry temperaments. The table below provides a list of the practical ministry gifts used in the *GraceGifts* assessment.

Practical Ministry Gifts

Administration	Evangelism	Intercessory Prayer	Pastor
Creativity	Exhortation	Leadership	Stewardship
Discerning of Spirits	Faith	Musical/Worship	Teacher
Disciple Maker	Giving	New Ministry	Wisdom
Encouragement	Helps/Service	Developer	

From the moment of our conception, God has been actively involved in the development of our natural and spiritual giftedness. This process culminates in full ministry expression once we are devoted to Christ and to His mission for our lives. When we accept Christ as our personal Savior and allow the Holy Spirit full reign within our lives, He begins a process that reclaims every aspect of our lives for Christ's purposes.

This process transforms our values, priorities and sense of self-worth, inspiring us with a renewed sense of value and purpose. It also transforms our natural skills, blessing those skills with renewed and expanded abilities when focused upon Kingdom purposes. Because of the close association between the natural skills God has already given us and the practical spiritual gifts He is now developing within us, we are able to practice and improve upon our giftedness. For example, with experience and ministry training, we can learn to become better teachers, encouragers, administrators, leaders, stewards, etc.

I liken the spiritual gifting process to the growth of a flower. Over time, the seed is sown and the plant begins to grow and take root. Only when the time is right, however, does the bud of the flower explode into full beauty and expression.

PRACTICAL GIFTS

The Holy Spirit augments our natural giftedness, transforming our skills into true spiritual gifts.

Your natural giftedness has been growing like a flower for many years. However, now that you are in Christ, God desires to take your natural giftedness to a whole new level of expression and beauty. The full expression of your natural giftedness will result in significant ministry impact within this world, bringing glory to God rather than yourself.

Assessment Limitations

Ministry leaders commonly use some form of spiritual gift assessment to help them objectively discern the potential giftedness within their congregations. However these spiritual gift assessments and their application generally have several serious flaws.

First, spiritual gift assessments are nothing more than interest and experience surveys. The assumption behind these assessments is that each person will express a natural interest in the areas in which God is working within his or her life. While this assumption is often accurate, it does not take into account human curiosity.

> Your natural giftedness has been growing like a flower for many years. However, now that you are in Christ, God desires to take your giftedness to a new level of expression and beauty.

Just because you and I may be curious about some aspect of spiritual life does not mean that we are skilled and gifted by God to serve in that area. It is not curiosity that defines how we should be mobilized for ministry but rather true spiritual giftedness. A high score on a spiritual gift assessment may or may not be an indication that the person is truly gifted. Spiritual giftedness must be tested within the body of Christ and affirmed by ministry leaders to determine its validity.

In one of my previous ministry ventures, a church that had been abandoned by its founding pastor contracted me to help determine its future direction. This church had an established contemporary worship team. Each week as I listened to the musicians and singers, I noticed that there were two female vocalists, yet I was only able to hear one female voice. When I addressed the matter with the sound engineers, I was informed that one of the female singers, Nancy, could not sing. While Nancy loved singing, and her heart made a joyful noise unto the Lord, she could not find a note no matter how hard she tried.

The way the church had been dealing with this matter was to simply turn off her microphone so that no one could hear her. The church board was fully aware of the situation but did not want to hurt Nancy by telling her that she was not gifted in leading worship. Instead they literally lied to her week after week, affirming her "interest" as a "spiritual gift." This was not a healthy or appropriate way to mobilize spiritual giftedness within the body of Christ.

Furthermore, by affirming Nancy within a ministry area for which she was not gifted, the church leadership was keeping her from serving in the area in which she was properly gifted. Through conversations with Nancy, we discovered that God had created her to be a prayer warrior. She had only stayed on the worship team because she did not want to let anyone down!

A second limitation of most spiritual gift assessments is that they do not take into account how a spiritual gift is filtered through an individual's personality. For example, let's suppose that two people in your church both received a high score on their spiritual gift assessment for "teaching." Jerry has a highly relational personality style and loves interpersonal interaction. John has a highly task-oriented personality style; he has a driven and dominant personality. Which person should be mobilized as a small group leader? The answer should be obvious. Jerry's personality lends itself to teaching small groups of people, whereas John would be better suited for a classroom or corporate teaching position.

Not long ago, Tamara and I decided to become members of a local ministry because of its focus on reaching young adults. For the first year we intentionally did not get very involved in serving because we wanted to build relationships and trust. One of the deacons suggested that we should volunteer as Welcome Center hosts, because this would enable us to meet a lot of people. Yet both Tamara and I possess personalities that prefer fewer, deeper relationships; we are very uncomfortable making "small-talk." While the deacon had good intentions, that area of service was not a good fit for our God-given ministry temperaments. We politely declined the offer.

If we fail to filter the practical spiritual gifts through each person's unique personality type, we will likely mobilize people for ministry in a manner that is inappropriate for them. The result can be devastating to the ministry as well as to those who want to serve.

A third flaw in spiritual gift assessments is that ministry leaders often assume that people with high scores in various gift areas are already equipped to use these gifts to serve the body of Christ. While at times this may be true, most lay people have had little or no training in how to use their gifts in ministry. Even when people claim to have prior ministry experience in particular gifts, it should not be assumed that they served effectively. Leaders are often too quick to move people into roles in order to fill perceived gaps in the overall ministry. Without appropriate equipping from spiritual leadership, this can be a setup for failure. If we wish to maximize our ministry impact potential, we must insist that our church leaders give ministry candidates appropriate training and preparation (see Eph. 4:12).

Mike is a good example of how giftedness can flourish with appropriate training. Mike was a new convert who had come into a relationship with Jesus Christ through one of my previous ministries. While he attended church rather faithfully, he always hid in the back of the auditorium and seldom participated in Bible studies. I was afraid his withdrawal might be due to a spiritual problem, so I met him for lunch to discuss it.

Mike confessed that he stayed in the background and did not attend Bible studies because he had never learned to read. To address this issue, I paired Mike up with one of our elders for regular one-on-one mentoring which included helping him learn to read. Since they used the Bible in the reading program, it also equipped him spiritually. Within five years, Mike not only could read, but he had assumed the position of deacon in the church.

Mike might never have realized his ministry potential had he not been properly equipped to fulfill God's mission for his life. He always had a big heart and loved to serve others, but for his servant-heart to truly flower, he needed to be equipped practically and spiritually for ministry.

Revelatory Giftedness

A second category of spiritual giftedness is strictly revelatory in nature. In other words, God "reveals" them *through* us only at the moment the specific gifts are needed. The revelatory gifts are distinctly different in nature from the practical ministry gifts. While the practical gifts are augmentations of our created nature and their use is filtered through our personalities, revelatory gifts are used in the moment as directed by the Holy Spirit. For example, a Christ-follower may have a sudden and overwhelming impression from God to pray over someone for their healing, and God answers the prayer, often dramatically.

The Christ-follower may or may not ever again be able to repeat the use of such a miraculous gift. Nor does his or her personality dictate how the prayer for healing should occur. When referring to revelatory gifts, it may be more accurate to communicate that "God has used me to heal others," rather than "I have the gift of healing."

> The revelatory gifts are distinctly different in nature from the practical ministry gifts. While the practical gifts are augmentations of our created nature and their use is filtered through our personalities, revelatory gifts are used in the moment as directed by the Holy Spirit.

Revelatory gifts are not something that we can possess. They are not natural to our humanity. These "grace gifts" are extended to us in such a manner that human beings can never take credit for them. They are clear and unadulterated penetrations of the divine into our fallen world. Revelatory gifts may include healing, miracles, word of knowledge, prophecy, speaking in tongues (publicly) and the interpretation of tongues. Some theologians also include exorcism in the revelatory list.

As with all spiritual gifts, revelatory gifts exist to uplift and benefit the body of Christ (1 Cor. 12:7). My Spanish mentor in college, who served for many years as a missionary in Central America, shared with me the following illustration of how the revelatory gift of tongues had been used to encourage him in his early ministry.

Paul had recently graduated from seminary, and found himself in the remote regions of Guatemala. What began as a grand missionary adventure had devolved into a lonely and frustrating experience; he had become lonely, sad and depressed. He could not see how he was making any difference in the lives of the Guatemalan tribes.

One Sunday morning as his small rural congregation met for church, an elderly woman began to speak in the middle of the service. The words she spoke, in perfect English, encouraged and comforted Paul. He told me that he was completely surprised by what she said, because her words addressed the core of his personal and spiritual struggles.

After the service was finished, Paul approached the woman to thank her for her kind words, only to discover that this uneducated woman could not speak a single word of English. God had used the public gift of tongues, through an uneducated elderly woman, for the "common good" of the missionary and the people to whom he was called to minister.

Revelatory gifts are commonly referred to as "self-evident" gifts because God has either worked such miracles in and through your life or He has not. Obviously, if He has, you would be aware of it. For this reason, many church leaders believe it is only necessary to assess for practical ministry giftedness.

The GraceGifts Assessment Tool

Within the AssessMe.org and E-Church Essentials programs, the default settings allow for assessment of the practical gifts only. If your ministry has established a ministry account with AssessMe.org or E-Church Essentials, your account administrator may modify the default setting to include the extended gift list. All of the *GraceGifts*© categories are listed in the table below; complete reports may be found in Appendix D.

GraceGifts Categories

Practical Gift List		Extended Gift List
Administration	Helps/Service	Exorcism
Creativity	Intercessory Prayer	Healing
Discerning of Spirits	Leadership	Word of Knowledge
Disciple Maker	Musical/Worship	Prophecy
Encouragement	New Ministry Developer	Speaking Publicly in Tongues
Evangelism	Pastor	Interpretation of Tongues
Exhortation	Stewardship	
Faith	Teacher	
Giving	Wisdom	

Although this gift list may vary from the list you or your pastoral leadership has grown accustomed to using, every attempt has been made to ensure a sound Biblical foundation for the gift labels as well as their related reports.

Do not assume that any assessment tool, particularly a spiritual gift inventory, accurately portrays an individual's true ministry nature. Spiritual giftedness must be tested within the body of Christ and affirmed by ministry leaders to determine its validity. This verification process generally occurs through personal interviews and observation of each ministry candidate in real-life ministry context. In addition, pastoral leaders may use the interview time to communicate their personal theological interpretations and applications regarding the various assessment reports.

GraceGifts© Overview

After completing the online *GraceGifts©* spiritual gift assessment, complete the worksheet below. As an aid to the development of your personal life mission plan, please focus your attention upon your practical spiritual gifts—those gifts which are Holy Spirit-inspired augmentations of the abilities that God ordained to be a part of your created nature.

Instructions

1. Go to www.assessme.org and take the *GraceGifts©* spiritual gift assessment.
2. Print your Spiritual Gifts assessment report or refer to your Spiritual Gifts report in Appendix D. (Note: The appendix includes reports for all of the *GraceGifts©*.)
3. Use your report information to help you complete the worksheet questions on the next page.

Worksheet

A. I affirm that my top spiritual gift is: _____

    1. I believe that God is calling me to apply this gift in the following area(s): _____

       _____

       _____

    2. This gift has been confirmed in my life by:_____

       _____

       _____

B. I affirm that my second top spiritual gift is: _____

    1. I believe that God is calling me to apply this gift in the following area(s): _____

       _____

       _____

    2. This gift has been confirmed in my life by:_____

       _____

       _____

C. I affirm that my third top spiritual gift is: _____

    1. I believe that God is calling me to apply this gift in the following area(s): _____

       _____

       _____

    2. This gift has been confirmed in my life by:_____

       _____

       _____

Chapter 8

Mentoring for Ministry Success

The Bible directs that before candidates are commissioned for ministry, church leaders should test and affirm their giftedness and readiness. In First Timothy 3:10, the Apostle Paul instructs that "deacons must first be tested; and then if there is nothing against them, let them serve." While this passage has traditionally been applied to the formal office of deacon within the local church, I believe we do a disservice to the body of Christ if we apply this passage too narrowly.

The Greek word "diakonos" (deacon) can be translated as "a servant of someone; a helper" as well as "an official or servant within the church." In Romans 16:1, Paul commends Phoebe to the Romans as a "servant of the church" in Cenchrea. In a very real sense, every person commissioned for ministry within the local church is functioning, like Phoebe, as a servant. Wisdom dictates that all servants should be held to the same standard. Failure to test people for ministry fitness inevitably damages the ministry organization and the people it serves.

What does a servant-testing plan look like? Scripture does not give us specifics. While many models exist and are generally appropriate, I suggest that an ideal strategy for developing and testing candidates include the following:

"Deacons [servants] must first be tested" (1 Tim. 3:10). Failure to test people for ministry fitness inevitably damages the ministry organization and the people it serves.

1. An assessment of *spiritual formation* to ensure that the candidate is, at the very least, rooted in the faith and the basics of sound doctrine. The level of spiritual maturity required will depend on the level of spiritual responsibility associated with the position.
2. Consideration of how *God uniquely designed the candidate for ministry*, including an assessment of his or her ministry temperament, leadership style, spiritual gifts, interests, passions and skills.
3. A process for *mentoring each candidate* according to their unique leadership style and ministry passions.

The primary goal of this chapter is to present one viable mentorship model that churches may use with their candidates to ensure a balance of training, testing and affirmation of each individual for ministry service.

Remember the principle of *mission myopia*? People will naturally gather around them others who are similar to themselves. In the context of leadership development, this principle implies that candidates will benefit most when they receive mentorship from proven leaders who share their leadership values and abilities. For example, visionary, task-oriented individuals will learn best from other visionary, task-oriented leaders.

The principle of mission myopia, when combined with the Leadership Style Assessment, suggests that ministry candidates may be directed to one of three distinct leadership development tracks: *Builder, Manager* or *Nurturer*. Each one of these tracks has very distinct leadership values which make cross-track training virtually impossible. The illustration on the next page summarizes these leadership values.

Leadership Styles

BUILDER	MANAGER	NURTURER
Independent ◀RELATIONAL CONTINUUM▶ Social		
Pioneer ▶ Strategic ▶ Administrator ▶ Team Leader ▶ Pastor ▶ Encourager		
• Visionary	• Motivational	• Relational
• Task Dominant	• Mission Tasks	• People Dominant
• Strategic	• Accomplishments	• Harmony
• Entreprenurial	• Administrative	• Pastoral
Influences others by developing systems, organizations, and programs that enable other people to serve effectively.	Influences others to accomplish a mission by providing resources, organization, and motivation.	Influences others through relationships that support and encourage.

Getting On Track

Have you ever considered that Jesus mentored each of His twelve disciples differently? Certainly Jesus held group training sessions, but His interpersonal interactions were unique with each disciple. He also invested more in Peter, James and John, His "inner circle," than the other disciples. The Apostle Paul recognized the special positions held by Peter, James and John, referring to them as the "pillars" of the church (Gal. 2:9). When we consider the ministry temperaments of each of these men, it becomes evident that Jesus was investing in his own three-strand-cord leadership team.

The Builder Track (Case Study: Peter)

Peter was the first disciple Jesus called to follow Him (Matt. 4:19). Peter exemplifies the "Builder" profile: he was a brash risk-taker—the most forceful, vocal and dominant personality among the twelve disciples. Peter was the one who risked stepping out of the boat to walk toward Jesus on the water (Matt. 14:28). During the transfiguration of Jesus on the mountain, it was Peter who blurted out his desire to build worship-shelters for Jesus, Moses and Elijah (Matt. 17:4). At the time of Christ's betrayal, Peter used his sword to cut off the ear of the high priest's servant (John 18:10). Peter was one of the few bold enough to follow and observe Jesus' trial and humiliation (John 18:15ff).

All Biblical references relating to Peter portray him as a strong, dominant leader. Jesus acknowledged Peter's "Builder" personality when He commissioned him: "And I tell you that you are Peter, and on this rock [the name Peter can be interpreted as "rock"] I will *build* my church, and the gates of Hades will not overcome it" (Matt. 16:18). Church history tells us that Peter indeed became the head of the church based in Jerusalem.

Training and Testing Builders

People who most identify with Peter likely share his Builder profile. Like Peter, today's Builders are commonly bold, brash, headstrong, entrepreneurial risk-takers. All Builders share a common passion to develop new ministries and a common motivation to initiate and complete a noble vision. Managers and Nurturers cannot identify with the creative passion that burns within the hearts of a Builder. If anything, Managers try to "manage" the Builder's passion to restrain and control it, and Nurturers try to repress the Builder's passion for fear that it may offend others.

When Managers or Nurturers attempt to mentor Builders, the Builders generally become frustrated and may disregard or devalue what they seek to offer. Often Builders strike off on their own, leaving Managers and Nurturers behind. This unfortunate consequence encourages Managers and Nurturers to label Builders as "independent" or "rebellious." Meanwhile, Builders often feel that Managers and Nurturers want to obstruct or control their noble ministry efforts.

Such misunderstandings could be alleviated considerably if mature Builders, who have learned to value Managers and Nurturers, are in charge of mentoring and developing Student-Builders. The table on the next page lists suggested topics that may be appropriate when equipping Student-Builders for service. Many of these mentorship categories are unique to ministry leaders who possess a Builder category profile. The Student-Builder will need to observe, assist and practice these valuable ministry mobilization arts.

Leadership Development Plan: Builder	

Vision casting
Strategic planning
Team member recruitment
Team member training, positioning
   and empowerment
Succession planning
The valuation and respect for
   non-Builder leadership styles
	Developing healthy authority and
	   accountability structures
	Patience: Learn to wait upon the
	   Holy Spirit before acting
	Receiving and valuing wise counsel
	Balancing priorities: Don't sacrifice family
	   or spiritual health for the mission

The Manager Track (Case Study: James)

People who possess a leadership style within the Manager Track (i.e., Administrator or Team Leader) excel at managing the tasks and people associated with a mission. While Peter was the *Builder*, James very likely was the *Manager*.

Not much is known regarding James. James did not write profusely as did Peter or John, and so it is difficult to be definitive regarding his nature. However we catch little glimpses of his leadership style through various Biblical passages.

The first major reference to James is recorded in Matthew 20:20–22. Here we find that the mother of James and John approached Jesus with a request that her two sons be permitted to be enthroned on the left and right of Jesus when he came into His kingdom. I find it interesting that James and John used their mother to make this request; a Peter personality would not have been so subtle. Mark 3:17 tells us that James was called a "[Son] of Thunder." In light of other Biblical references regarding James, this reference suggests that he had a passion to accomplish tasks associated with a mission.

Yet it is not until the birth of the church that we begin to clearly perceive James' leadership style as a Manager. When the apostles at the Council of Jerusalem were debating whether traditional Jewish laws must apply to Gentile Christians, James listened to all of the arguments, then provided a framework for consensus and action:

> It is my judgment, therefore, that we should not make it difficult for the Gentiles who are turning to God. Instead we should write to them, telling them to abstain from food polluted by idols, from sexual immorality, from the meat of strangled animals and from blood. For Moses has been preached in every city from the earliest times and is read in the synagogues on every Sabbath. (Acts 15:19–21)

In this declaration at the Jerusalem Council, James shows himself to be an administrative leader. He not only perceived the problem at hand but devised a solution and inspired the Council to take appropriate action.

Training and Testing Mangers

People with Manager leadership styles are highly skilled at addressing the task and human resource issues associated with any mission. The Manager track consists of people who value practical solutions to practical problems. They do not typically have the Builder's entrepreneurial nature or the Nurturer's skill in pastoral care, but they are crucial to the efficiency and effectiveness of all ministry organizations.

When developing and testing ministry candidates within

the Manager track, it is important to identify whether the candidate's leadership preference is for task-management (Administrative Leadership) or people-management (Team Leadership). The candidate's development and testing program should be customized according to their preferred management style. The table below lists suggested topics that may be appropriate when equipping Student-Managers for ministry service. The Student-Manager will need to observe, assist and practice these valuable ministry mobilization arts.

Leadership Development Plan: Manager	
Administrative Leader Track	Team Leader Track
Delegation skills	Preventing pride through accountability
Defining realistic task timelines	Sticking with a strategic plan
Balancing tasks with relationships	Submission to authorities
Avoiding obstructionist behaviors	Honor the pioneering leaders
Shared Training Objectives	
Project management	
Identifying strategic priorities and completing identified tasks	
Record keeping and reporting of quantitative/qualitative mission results	
Recruiting and assigning people to functional roles	
Resource/equip people for successful ministry service	
Ministry accountability: confrontation and conflict management	

The Nurturer Track (Case Study: John)

John is the epitome of the Nurturing leader. In his writings he speaks of "love" at least sixty times. John's over-arching theme is that God is love, and because of His love toward us, we should love one another. John's Gospel and his letters are by far the most pastoral writings found in the New Testament.

John was the younger brother of James, and this birth-order may help explain the differences between the two brothers. Although sociologists and psychologists may disagree regarding birth-order dynamics, it is generally accepted that older siblings tend to be more aggressive and task oriented, while younger siblings tend to be more relationally sensitive.

John's unique way of referring to himself within his Gospel conveys his Nurturing nature; he calls himself "the disciple Jesus loved." This title was John's way of communicating self-awareness regarding his relationship with his Savior and Lord—that Jesus loved John so much that He would suffer and die for him. It was not a title intended to elevate his status over that of the other disciples, as if Jesus loved John more than Peter or James. And it certainly was not a homosexual reference, as some radical theologians and film producers have suggested.

In John 19:26 we find an incredible pastoral care picture! Only John, and no other disciple, stands with Jesus' mother at the foot of the cross. We find him supporting and comforting Mary as her Son suffers and dies. Jesus looks down from the cross and sees His mother, whom He naturally loves, being cared for by the "disciple He loves." He acknowledges John's nurturing nature and commissions him to take care of Mary as if he were her son.

Training and Testing Nurturers

As we have already learned, people with a leadership style in the Nurturer category tend to devalue tasks and mission.

They highly value interpersonal relationships. It is in their nature to stand at the foot of the Cross and give comfort to those who grieve. They empathize with those in pain and rejoice with those who rejoice. The Nurturing leader is uniquely empathic, able to share the spiritual and emotional issues experienced by others.

Because the Builder and Manager leadership styles are predominantly task-oriented, individuals from these categories are ill-equipped to train people for relational ministry. Student-Nurturers are best mentored by proven Nurturing Leaders. The table below lists suggested topics that may be appropriate when equipping Student-Nurturers for ministry service. The Student-Nurturer will need to observe, assist and practice these valuable ministry mobilization arts.

Leadership Development Plan: Nurturer	
Pastoral care	Basic counseling skills
Visitation of the sick (hospital visitation)	Small group training
Intercessory prayer and anointing with oil	One-on-one discipleship training
Listening skills	Recovery ministry training

Summary

I believe a "one-size-fits-all" testing and training strategy is entirely insufficient when preparing candidates for ministry service. We have learned that each leadership category—Builder, Manager and Administrator—has a unique set of values and mission focus.

Mentors can only give to others what they themselves possess. As a result, cross-track training is virtually impossible.

While it is important that we value diversity when building leadership teams, because differing leadership styles add valuable perspectives and skills that complement each other, leadership training requires that mentors serve out of their areas of expertise. Mentors can only give to others what they themselves possess. As a result, cross-track training is virtually impossible.

I challenge church leaders to develop an intentional three-track leadership training and testing program within their church ministry. The illustration on the next page provides a flow chart that you may find helpful in implementing a mentorship program.

I believe this program, when properly implemented, will revolutionize your church's ability to minister effectively and maximize your potential pool of ministry candidates.

Ministry candidates, I encourage you to find a church that offers a leadership training program appropriate to your unique development needs. If this is not possible, find a mentor who shares your leadership style and ministry passions to appropriately guide and affirm your ministry development.

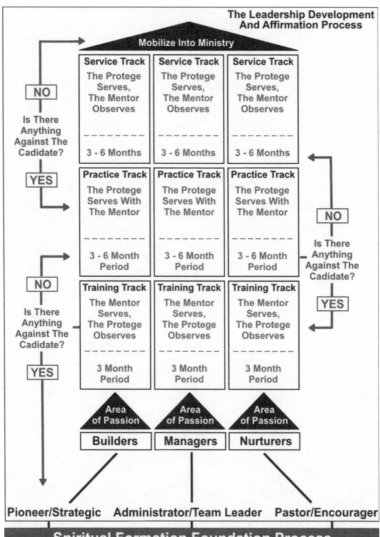

Chapter 9

The Ministry-
Mobilization Filter

I must confess that one of my vices is coffee—the stronger the better. However I have found that poorly-filtered coffee is not enjoyable. One summer on a family camping trip, I tried to make coffee over the fire pit by heating coffee grounds and water in a campfire coffeepot, then pouring the liquid into my cup through a paper towel. My makeshift filter did not work well. The grit of the grounds floating in my coffee and laying in the bottom of my cup seriously detracted from the coffee experience. Good filters make good coffee.

The same may be said of the ministry-mobilization "filter" process. If we effectively apply all the principles that we have covered in this book, we will filter out misperceptions that distract us from accomplishing our true mission objectives and refine our focus regarding how God truly desires us to serve Him. Effective filters make effective "missionaries."

Yet church leaders consistently want to shortcut the filtering process. It is very common for them to position people into ministry roles based solely upon the candidate's assessed spiritual gifts, without taking into account their spiritual health and unique design for ministry. When ministry leaders shortcut the filtering process in this way, they may temporarily plug holes in their ministry organizations, but they will never help people accomplish the mission for which they were created.

When ministry leaders shortcut the filtering process in this way, they may temporarily plug holes in their ministry organizations, but they will never help people accomplish the mission for which they were created.

The filtering process is a refining process. "Refinement" is a dominant Biblical theme that applies not only to our spiritual condition but also to our ministry preparation.

There is a tight relationship between our spiritual health and our personal ministry. We lack the impetus to serve effectively when we are spiritually weak. Similarly, we cannot claim to be spiritually mature and yet fail to serve our Lord in ministry.

The Apostle Paul emphasizes the interconnection of these two themes when he instructs Timothy: "In a large house there are articles not only of gold and silver, but also of wood and clay; some are for noble purposes and some for ignoble. If a man cleanses himself from the latter, he will be an instrument for noble purposes, made holy, *useful to the Master and prepared to do any good work*" (2 Tim. 2:20–21).

Your mission *is* the "good work" for which you have been created. In your pursuit to identify your life mission, you have so far taken numerous assessments and explored many topics. It is now time to begin pulling all of these pieces together into a cohesive ministry-mobilization strategy. This strategy will enable you to identify ministry qualities that God would deem as "noble" and filter out personal qualities that he would deem "ignoble."

The Mission-Mobilization Filter Process

In practical real-life application, the order in which people address the various filter elements may vary. However, the linear filter process depicted in the illustration on the next page can be utilized in most cases.

Mission Mobilization Filter

**MADE FOR
A MISSION**

1 **SPIRITUAL
FORMATION**
*Your Spiritual
Maturity & Health*

2 **ePERSONALITY**
*Your Ministry
Temperament*

3 **LEADERSHIP
STYLE**
*How You
Influence Others*

4 **GRACE*GIFTS***
*Your Practical
Spiritual Gifts*

5 **SKILLS**
*Your Interests,
Passions & Skills*

**REFINED
FOR A
MISSION**

"If a man cleanses himself of the
latter, he will be an instrument for
noble purposes, made holy, useful
to the Master and prepared to do
any good work"

2 Timothy 2:20-21

Spiritual Formation Filter:
Your Spiritual Maturity and Health

The filtering process begins with your relationship with Jesus Christ. You can only receive a commission for ministry from God once you have received Jesus Christ as your Lord and Savior. The Apostle Paul explains: "Therefore, if anyone is in Christ, he is a new creation; the old has gone, the new has come! All this is from God, who [first] reconciled us to himself through Christ *and [then] gave us the ministry of reconciliation*" (2 Cor. 5:17–18).

From God's perspective, when you came to faith in Christ, you instantly became a new creation. However, as you live your life, you are also in a process of daily becoming that new creation. Theologians call this principle the "now and the not yet." Your motivation for becoming and living the "new creation" life must be your authentic love for Christ. Christ's love is the only legitimate compelling force that can inspire within you a desire to relate to Him and to serve Him. For this reason, your daily relationship with God must always precede your ministry for God. God does not desire your ministry sacrifices; He desires your heart. Once He has your heart, He can direct it to accomplish great things for the kingdom of Christ.

The first ministry mobilization filter, *Spiritual Formation*, is an honest evaluation of your present spiritual health and vitality. You cannot perceive yourself or your ministry mission correctly apart from a growing appreciation of being a "new creation" in Christ. The moment you became a new creation, you were also commissioned to participate in Christ's "ministry of reconciliation." Of course this does not mean that at this point you are spiritually prepared to serve. Your spiritual formation process is a lifelong "boot camp" consisting of continual self-examination and spiritual training, so that you may be fit and ready to serve God as He leads.

ePersonality Filter: Your Ministry Temperament

The second ministry mobilization filter, *ePersonality*, enables you to appreciate your ministry temperament. As you have learned in the course of reading this book, your personality type defines the manner in which you will serve your Lord. You possess a ministry temperament that is ideally suited for the function that God created you to perform. Through the ePersonality filter, you learned that your heart cries out to serve your God with a unique passion, summarized in a "Heart's Cry Statement." You also learned about the personal strengths and weaknesses of your ministry temperament and came to understand that your ministry mission will require you to utilize your strengths and allow others to come alongside to support you in your weaknesses. By serving according to your strengths, you honor the person God created you to be, maximize your ministry-impact potential, and minimize stress and fatigue that would threaten to dissuade you from the accomplishment of your mission.

Leadership Style Filter: How You Influence Others

The third ministry mobilization filter, *Leadership Style*, helps you focus your ministry energies even further by identifying your preferred method of influencing others through direct interpersonal ministry. Your leadership style is designed by God to emulate the functional ministry of either God the Father, God the Son, or God the Holy Spirit. God created you in His image. In Genesis 1:26 God says, "Let *us* make man in *our* image, in *our* likeness." The use of plural pronouns in this passage does not imply that we have three gods. God is one. However, God expresses Himself in three distinct personalities. Likewise, you are made in God's image to be an expression of His nature.

It is crucial that you learn to express yourself in ministry service according to the aspect of God's nature that He intended for you. It is natural for you to possess attributes that may be identified with any or all the members of the Godhead. The purpose of the Leadership Style filter is to identify the member of the Godhead that most closely depicts your ministry nature. Do you primarily emulate the Administrative/ Strategic Planner nature of God the Father, the Team Leader/ Pioneer nature of God the Son, or the Pastoral/ Encourager nature of God the Holy Spirit? Once you can identify clearly with your spiritual role-model, you will have the ability to excel in those ministry opportunities that honor the person God made you to be, and to say "no" to those ministry opportunities that would be better served by an individual with a differing leadership style.

GraceGifts Filter: Your Practical Spiritual Gifts

The fourth ministry mobilization filter, *GraceGifts*, helps you identify and develop the specific spiritual gifts that God has instilled in your life. Your gifts must be interpreted in light of your leadership style and ministry temperament (i.e., personality). Remember, how you utilize your practical ministry gifts is always determined by your unique personality dynamics. For this reason, you will be encouraged to generate a "mission clarification statement" for each one of your dominant spiritual gifts, taking your ministry temperament and leadership style into account. This process will help you see more clearly how you should use your gifts.

Skills Filter: Your Interests, Passions and Skills

The fifth and final filter challenges you to reinterpret your various interests, passions and skills from a mission focus rather than a career focus. A mission focus will answer four values-based questions:

1. **What is my primary goal?** (i.e., making disciples of Christ)
2. **What is my primary focus?** (i.e., using my abilities to serve the needs of others)
3. **How will I measure success?** (i.e., by whether I have been obedient to God's leading and empowerment)
4. **What is my faith focus?** (i.e., reliance upon the Holy Spirit)

How you respond to these questions will likely have a profound impact upon every aspect of your life, including the decisions you make, how you invest your time and resources, and the relationships you establish. The fundamental goal is to live life intentionally, positioning your life to maximize your ministry impact.

Summary

Each of these filters provides a framework and tools to assist you in clarifying the mission God intends for your life.

Yet, as with all tools, the care by which they are used will determine their effectiveness. I challenge you to bathe this process in prayer, seeking confirmation of your mission first from God and secondly from godly people. The sum total of all this information will allow you, with God's help, to identify a specific ministry mission that is ideally suited for your current level of spiritual maturity, unique nature, stage of life and understanding of God's leading or "ministry calling." After all, you were made for a mission!

Chapter 10

Writing Your Life Mission Plan

In this chapter you will prepare a personalized life mission plan. After reflecting on the worksheets from previous chapters, you will revise and refine your responses and then write a final draft of your life mission plan in your own words. Do not rush this process; take time to prayerfully work through each step.

You may find it helpful to discuss the various steps with those closest to you in order to gain their insights and perspectives. These people can be a support to you in the months and years to come, encouraging you to "stay the course" as defined by your life mission plan. I pray that God will use you in incredible ways, for His glory and the benefit of Christ's kingdom, as you pursue your life mission plan.

Life Mission Plan Worksheet

Date Completed: _____

1. Spiritual Formation: My Spiritual Maturity and Health

Review the worksheets you completed in chapter 1 and your Felt Need Report in Appendix A to help you draft your felt need and spiritual formation statements. In six months, gauge your progress and revise these statements as necessary. You may wish to make this process an on-going spiritual formation discipline.

Felt Need Statement:

I feel my most immediate need is to love the Lord my God with all of my _____.
(Heart/Soul/Mind/Strength)

I recognize that until I address my felt need, it may become a roadblock to my spiritual development and ministry mission. I believe God is calling me to address the following felt-need issues in my life and ministry: _____

_____

_____

_____

_____
(Summarize and personalize your Felt Need Report)

Spiritual Formation Statement:

To help me grow in my spiritual maturity and health, over the next six months I will seek to address the following areas through prayer, the empowerment of the Holy Spirit and the support of my pastor or small group: _____

_____

_____

_____

_____

(Summarize your top 1–3 spiritual formation goals)

2. ePersonality: My Ministry Temperament

Review the worksheets you completed in chapter 2, along with your ePersonality Report in Appendix B to help you draft your ministry temperament and application statements.

Ministry Temperament Statement:

Because God gave me a _____ ministry temperament,
my heart's cry is _____
             (Profile title)

_____

(Put your heart's cry statement in your own words)

I affirm that God uniquely designed me to primarily relate
to people _____,
         (Independently/Relationally)
process information _____
            (Abstractly/Concretely)
process decisions with my _____
           (Head/Heart)
and relate to the world around me _____.
           (Systematically/Adaptively)

In summary, God uniquely created me with a ministry temperament designed to: _____

_____

_____

_____

(Summarize your ePersonality profile in your own words)

Application Statement:

If I am to honor who God made me to be, I should seek ministry opportunities that require _____

_____

and say "No" to ministry opportunities that require _____

_____

_____ .

3. Leadership Style: How I Influence Others
   Review the worksheets you completed in chapters 5 and 6, and your Leadership Style Report in Appendix C, to help you draft your leadership style and succession planning statements.

Leadership Style Statement:

Because God gave me a _____ leadership style,
(Profile title)
I primarily influence others by _____

_____

_____

_____
(Summarize your Leadership Style profile in your own words)

My leadership style most closely emulates my _____
(Heavenly Father/Savior/ Paraclete)
who is my ideal role model for ministry. If I am to maximize the success of my ministry mission, I should seek to partner with a _____ Leader and a _____Leader.
    (Complementary style)   (Complementary style)

Succession Planning Statement:

I have identified _____ as a (potential)
           (Mentor's name)

mentor who shares my leadership style category and can equip me to grow in ministry effectiveness. I have also identified

_____ as a (potential) ministry
(Ministry candidate's name)

candidate with a similar leadership style to my own, whom I can mentor and equip, helping him or her to grow in ministry effectiveness.

4. GraceGifts: My Practical Spiritual Gifts
    Review the worksheets you completed in chapter 7, and your GraceGifts© Report in Appendix C, to help you draft your GraceGifts© statement. For each of your top three practical spiritual gifts, include a "mission clarification statement" that explains how your ministry temperament and leadership style impact the application of your gift in ministry.

GraceGifts Statement:

Taking into account my ministry temperament and leadership style, I believe that God is calling me to apply my gift of

_____ in the following way:
(Top practical spiritual gift)

_____

_____,

my gift of _____ in the following way:
(Second top practical spiritual gift)

_____

_____,

and my gift of _____ in the following way:
(Third top practical spiritual gift)

_____

_____.

5. Skills: My Interests, Passions and Skills

    Review the worksheets you completed in chapter 4 to help you draft your ministry focus and passion statements. Note: the passion statement you developed will likely require revision now that you have a better understanding of your leadership style and spiritual gifts.

Ministry Focus Statement:

Based upon my growing awareness of God's *invocatio*—what He wishes to accomplish through me—I am committed to directing my primary interests, passions and skills to accomplish God's purposes and make a difference for the kingdom of Christ.

My primary goal is making disciples of Christ. I believe that my interests, passions and skills can facilitate this process by

_____

_____

_____

_____

(Explain how your interests, passions, and skills can support your disciple-making.)

My primary focus is serving the needs of others. I can use my interests, passions and skills to serve others by _____

_____

_____

_____

_____

_____

_____

(Explain how God is directing you to serve others with your interests, passions and skills.)

I will measure success by whether I have been obedient to God's leading and empowerment. I perceive that God is leading me to use my interests, passions and skills to _____

_____

_____

_____

_____

(Explain how you perceive God is leading you to use your interests, passions and skills.)

My faith focus is reliance upon the Holy Spirit. I anticipate that I will face the following faith challenges in my life and ministry: _____

_____

_____

_____

_____

(Explain any specific faith challenges you expect to encounter.)

I believe God desires for me to respond to these challenges by _____

_____

_____

(Explain how you will respond in faith.)

Passion Statement (Final draft): I am passionate about:

_____

_____

_____

(Revise first draft, based on additional understanding.)

I am confident that my passion for this ministry is inspired by the Holy Spirit because _____

_____

_____

_____

(Revise first draft, based on additional understanding.)

My passion for this ministry has been confirmed through

_____

_____

_____

_____

_____

(Revise first draft, based on additional understanding.)

Life Mission Plan

Use the space below to write your life mission plan, based on the worksheets completed earlier in this chapter. You should make an effort to use your own words as much as possible.

Date Completed: _____

_____

_____

_____

_____

_____

_____

_____

_____

_____

_____

_____

_____

_____

_____

_____

Felt Need Reports

The following Felt Need reports are also available in the "extras" portion of the AssessME.org website. (Also see chart on p. 36)

ABCD/DC - The Wounded Warrior Profile

People who identify with the Wounded Warrior profile have emotional and spiritual pain that makes it hard for them to develop relational intimacy and trust with God and others. Their pain may have been caused by a friend, a family member, or a trusted authority figure. It may also be the result of physical and emotional exhaustion; they have worked so hard and long in their own strength that they have "burned out" and lost their spiritual vitality.

Regardless of how the hurt occurred, if you identify with the Wounded Warrior profile you are probably feeling lonely, angry, exhausted, impatient, and distrustful of others. You may feel distant from God, despite being active in your church or ministry. Your devotional life may also suffer: you may find it difficult to pray, and your prayers tend to focus on your own needs. You may find it difficult to worship God or study the Bible. When asked to participate in ministry, you don't seem to have the energy or desire.

Unfortunately, you may distance yourself from the very relationships that could help restore you, mistakenly believing that "time heals all wounds" (in reality, unaddressed pain generally sows seeds of bitterness). Alternatively, you may over-compensate by trying to "please and appease" others—an unhealthy "servant attitude" that is motivated by a deep desire to win acceptance and avoid emotional or spiritual rejection.

These descriptions may appear quite negative, but there are positive attributes to this profile. First, your heart is emotionally and spiritually sensitive. You just need to recognize and resist Satan's attempts to re-direct that sensitivity away from God. King David was described as a "man after God's own heart." With healing, this could soon describe you. Second, though you may feel distant from God, you recognize the problem and desire to address the issues which are impeding your love-relationship with your Heavenly Father.

Your path to spiritual growth includes repenting of bitterness and self-justification, and forgiving those who may have hurt you. Don't wait for others to seek your forgiveness—they may not even be aware they have injured you. Nor do you necessarily need to make them aware of how they have hurt you—the Holy Spirit is more than capable of convicting them of their sin. Your responsibility is to simply forgive, even as God has forgiven you.

ADBC/CB – The Bondage Breaker Profile

Individuals who identify with the Bondage Breaker profile realize their need to mature in Christ and conform their actions to His purposes. They want to serve their Lord faithfully and with integrity, but the choices they have made or the emotional/spiritual pain they have suffered have kept them from growing in Christlikeness. Their actions to this point may have been anything but Christlike. They feel trapped and ill-equipped to overcome the problems guilt that have hindered their spiritual development. People who identify with the Bondage Breaker profile long to be free of the problems that dominate their private and public life, but are often unsure of the steps they need to take to receive spiritual and emotional freedom.

If you relate to this profile, hear what the Apostle Paul has to say: "It is for freedom that Christ has set us free. Stand firm, then, and do not let yourselves be burdened again by a yoke of slavery" (Gal. 5:1). It is time for you to move from bondage to freedom. Freedom in Christ involves developing a Christlike character, inner and relational forgiveness and healing, and sound scriptural training. Your day-to-day behaviors and your personal ministry must be founded in the Word of God and empowered by the Holy Spirit.

This kind of living requires a continual yielding of your will and desires to the Holy Spirit. Paul counsels us to "live by the Spirit, and you will not gratify the desires of the sinful nature. For the sinful nature desires what is contrary to the Spirit and the Spirit what is contrary to the sinful nature" (Gal. 5:16–17). Living "by the Spirit" means living under His guidance and control. Your challenge will be to respond to the Holy Spirit's leading and prompting, rather than charging forward in your own understanding.

It is also important to acknowledge the spiritual strongholds in your life, confessing them to God and seeking forgiveness and freedom from them. In some cases, it may help to share your spiritual stronghold issues with a pastor or small group that can support you in prayer and hold you accountable.

The positive attributes of the Bondage Breaker profile are a deep desire to relate intimately with God and to serve Him with all your strength. These are noble ambitions which honor the very purposes for which God created you.

BADC/CD – The At-Risk Profile

People who identify with the At-Risk profile feel distant from God and from many of their human relationships as well, usually due to emotional pain. Their pain may cause them to withdraw and put up walls of self-protection, which only deepen the pain and feelings of loneliness.

This profile is called "At-Risk" because to this point, Satan's strategies appear to have been working. If you relate to this profile, you continue to struggle with personal pain and may exhibit bitterness, sarcasm, anxiety, and despair. You may find yourself asking God "Why?" while blaming God for allowing the pain. In so judging God, you have lost sight of His loving character, gracious promises, and victorious power.

Satan wants you to believe that God did not love you enough or was not powerful enough to stop the pain in your life. You may feel that God has not shown Himself worthy of your faith and trust. And yet, deep inside, you desire to escape your spiritual bondage and learn to trust. You want God in your life. You can be encouraged by the fact that Satan attacks those who pose the greatest threat to him and hold potential for significant advancement of Christ's kingdom. With restoration and training, you may discover that God has significant plans for your life and ministry.

ACBD/DB – The Seeker Profile

People who identify with the Seeker Profile express a desire to grow in their love relationship with God and learn more about who He is and how to serve Him. People who identify with the Seeker Profile are usually wrestling with emotional and intellectual issues in their spiritual life. They commonly wonder why God allows difficulty in their lives. They may question whether God really cares for them or their situation. They may feel distant from God, but earnestly desire to remedy the relationship. This ongoing struggle may be a tension between their heart and their intellect.

If you identify with the Seeker profile, you probably know your relationship with God is not where it should be. You may have been trying to figure out for some time how to get "un-stuck" and get back on the right track in your relationship with God. You may sense that the first step to restoration and spiritual health is to heal your heart, but you may not know how to take the appropriate steps toward healing. As a Seeker, you desire guidance and information so that your spiritual life can be restored and once again move forward.

BCAD/DA – The Restoration Profile

People who identify with the Restoration profile may exhibit an inner spiritual life that has for some reason become lukewarm. They may lack the spiritual hunger and vitality they once possessed, having "left their first love" (Rev. 2:4 NASB). They are less concerned with ministry service than with getting their relationship with Christ back on track. In fact, their spiritual state may be a direct result of serving too hard, for too long, in their own strength. They seek balance in their life. They may require rest. They desire to be spiritually and emotionally restored.

If you identify with the Restoration profile, you may find that one aid to your spiritual restoration is to meditate upon the Word of God. You may already be quite Biblically literate if you have been walking with Christ for a number of years. In this case, your desire may not be to "learn more" about the Bible, but rather to allow God to speak with you and to direct your life and ministry more effectively.

Restoration is a very common theme in the Psalms. It may be beneficial for you to spend extended time meditating and praying through the Psalms. You will likely identify passionately with the raw emotional and spiritual struggles of the Psalmists.

BDAC/CA – The Transformational Profile

People who identify with the Transformational profile generally desire greater vitality and intimacy in their relationship with Jesus Christ. However, to reach that next relational level will require that they entrust significant areas of their life to God's control. Giving up control is never easy, but God wants all we have and all we are. Every Christ-follower soon learns that true change can only occur as we surrender our will to His will.

The work of the Holy Spirit is always loving and good for you, but not necessarily easy. Expect the Holy Spirit to challenge your current values and priorities—your ways are seldom His ways. You will learn that true transformation means dying to self—that is, sacrificing your old lifestyle and selfish ambitions—and learning to humbly allow Christ to rule in you and through you for His glory. The goal of the Holy Spirit is to transform your character to increasingly reflect the character of Jesus. This character transformation process is evidence that God is at work within you, and this evidence will enable you to trust Him to continue that work.

At this point in your spiritual development you may begin asking for the first time what God desires of your life rather than merely expecting God to bless your plans. You may also sense that God indeed does have a plan and purpose for your life, though you may not be sure what it is. If you have been walking with the Lord for a number of years, you may be aware of God's plan, but for whatever reason may have strayed from that divine purpose. It is time to repent and return once again to the mission for which you were created.

CABD/DB – The Inquirer Profile

People who identify with the Inquirer profile are wrestling with such matters as good versus evil, the problem of sin, and the character and authority of God. They have been trying to make sense of their life experiences. Their heart may cry out the proverbial question, "Why do bad things happen to good people?" They feel that if they only knew the answers to such questions, they could move forward in their life and faith, but at this point they are confused and unfulfilled. Inquirers tend to seek a rational/intellectual process to heal their heart and spirit, yet they may still struggle with feelings of bitterness, anger, anxiety, fear or regret. They may also find it difficult to truly forgive people.

If you identify with the Inquirer profile, there are answers to your many questions, and hope in a life guided by Jesus Christ. Your heart may have been wounded, but only through true surrender of those wounds to Jesus Christ will you find that "in all things God works for the good of those who love him, who have been called according to his purpose" (Rom. 8:28).

CBAD/DA – The Student Profile

People who identify with the Student profile believe that they need more information to adequately live in a vital and growing relationship with Jesus Christ. They may be seeking to understand the Bible so that they can decide if the Christian life is for them; they may already be committed to following Christ, but desire to learn more of the "how-to" of the Christian life. In either case, the Student will greatly benefit from spiritual mentors (e.g., pastors, small groups), as well as associations with other Students who are at the same stage in their spiritual life. Mentor-to-peer and peer-to-peer relationships are vitally important for the nurture of the Student's spiritual development.

If you see yourself in the Student profile, you need to discern the difference between knowing "about" Christ and living "in" Christ. Many Christ-followers are educated way beyond their level of life application. Healthy spiritual development occurs when you consistently apply what you know to be true. This is not a work of human effort alone, but is empowered by the Holy Spirit within you. The power of the Holy Spirit will enable you to consistently develop your intimacy *with* Christ, your personal character *in* Christ, and your personal ministry *for* Christ. Knowledge alone cannot nurture these fundamental spiritual formation practices, or help you know and relate to your God. Paul criticized the false teachers of his day for "always learning but never able to acknowledge the truth" (2 Tim. 3:7). Be careful not to make the same mistake. Knowledge is necessary, but by itself can result in arrogance and pride, while life application always requires submission and humility. Above all, God values a humble and contrite spirit.

CDAB/BA – The Apprentice Profile

People who identify with the Apprentice profile typically desire to learn more about what the Bible teaches, to better live the Christian life and serve Christ through ministry. They may currently feel that their knowledge of Scripture is limited. Apprentices can benefit from spiritual mentors and teachers who will help them learn and apply what they learn to their daily life and ministry. Their spiritual training could include a solid grounding in the teachings of Scripture, character formation to better reflect the nature of Christ, and preparation for ministry.

If you identify with the Apprentice profile, you probably want to *learn* more so you can *do* more for Christ. You may have spiritual leaders whom you respect and wish to emulate. This may be entirely appropriate—there is a reason this is called the Apprentice profile. You may find it beneficial to come under the guidance and instruction of a spiritual mentor. In fact, this is the rabbinical model given to us in Scripture; Jesus mentored His disciples, and they sought to become like Him in life and ministry. Select your mentor(s) carefully.

DABC/CB – The Character Profile

People who identify with the Character profile are generally concerned with their spiritual development. They desire to apply their faith in their daily Christian walk, and want their life to exemplify the character and nature of Jesus Christ. They may also be struggling to overcome obstacles of emotional pain and strongholds of sin that are keeping them from becoming what Christ desires them to be, so they may be dealing with guilt, shame and regret. If they have been hurt by others, they may also struggle with anger, anxiety, bitterness and distrust.

If you relate to this profile, be assured that Christ is faithful. He is committed to your spiritual and personal development. As you surrender areas of your life to Him, He promises to exchange your sin for *His* righteousness, your sorrow for *His* joy, and your shame for *His* glory! He who has forgiven you so much can empower you to forgive those who have sinned against you. As you learn to surrender every area of your life to the control of Christ, people will see the change in your behavior and words. You will also see the character and nature of Christ being revealed through your life. If you are serious about becoming the man or woman God desires you to be, you will find that the support and accountability of a spiritual mentor, pastor, or small group is crucial to helping you make significant changes in your life.

DBAC/CA – The Passion Profile

People who identify with the Passion profile generally desire God to work in and through them for significant Kingdom impact within this world. They generally relate to Christ with considerable passion and desire their life and ministry to be shaped by His presence and power. However, they may feel that they are not fully accomplishing their life's mission or achieving their potential in Christ. They may desire greater intimacy in their worship and prayer life. They may desire greater impact on others through their personal ministry. They generally wish to experience God fully within their lives and allow their lives to radiate the character, presence, and power of Jesus Christ. To mature appropriately and avoid the pitfalls of pride that can accompany such an ambitious desire, these people may benefit from the spiritual support and accountability of spiritual leaders they respect.

If you identify with the Passion profile, take care that your motives are pure. It can be easy to confuse pride and selfish ambition with a desire to be used by God. God†"opposes the proud but gives grace to the humble" (James 4:6). If there is pride in your life, you need to address it before your spiritual life and ministry can move forward. Seek the honest advice and evaluation of a trusted spiritual leader; often the things we are blind to are obvious to others.

DCAB/BA – The Action Profile

People who identify with the Action profile desire to get "plugged in" to ministry. They want to make a difference in this world. Their immediate goal is personal equipping for ministry and affirmation of their call to ministry. To be effective for Christ and His kingdom, they must first be mature in personal character, established in their understanding and application of God's Word, and affirmed for ministry by their spiritual leadership. They may be unsure of their divine mission in this world and require assistance from ministry leaders to help discern areas of giftedness and ministry calling.

If you identify with the Action profile, you should find a balance between *being* in Christ and *doing* for Christ. It is important to nurture your emotional and spiritual love-relationship with God. Do not allow yourself to become so busy serving God that you neglect your relationship with Him and fail to trust His guidance and empowerment for your ministry. Seek out spiritual leaders who will provide equipping, accountability, and support for your ministry development. This will help you avoid a lot of stress, anxiety and fatigue.

ePersonality Reports

The following reports are also available within the ePersonality assessment offered on-line from E-Church Essentials and AssessMe.org.

The Overseer

Heart's Cry Statement

Let me plan and manage projects and teams.

Highlights

- Strong implementation planners and managers
- Highly directive in administrative style
- Values and utilizes systems and structures
- May rely heavily on proven methods from the past
- Make excellent deacons, staff leaders and ministry leaders
- May require support in dealing with difficult interpersonal relationships

Who God Made You to Be

The Overseer is outgoing and wants to help people accomplish objectives. The Overseer is usually a logical implementation planner and manager who values gaining facts from the team and outside resources. The Overseer does not create vision and will not use vision to inspire people. The Overseer will receive a vision from respected and trusted authorities and create the systems and structures necessary to accomplish the given vision. The Overseer uses his or her outgoing personality, along with researched facts, to attract people and help them commit to the task at hand. However, once the facts are gathered and a plan is put into action, the Overseer may be inflexible to change the plan unless provided with overwhelming evidence to alter the Overseer's established perspective.

While Overseers are outgoing, they can lack sensitivity toward others. If an Overseer is not careful, he or she may be accused of pushing people to accomplish the objective. The Overseer can unintentionally act as if the *task* is of greater value than the *team*. An immature or stressed Overseer may seem to have a directive, almost dictatorial, spirit. Overseers usually do not have difficulty confronting people they believe are acting or serving inappropriately. They will be quick to make their expectations clear to their team.

Overseers typically adhere to the organization's established policies and value authority structures. In fact, they highly value the establishment of organizational structures. Where such systems are lacking, they may establish them if for no other reason than that they require them in order to be effective. If an established system is ineffective, Overseers will likely want to improve the system. They are effective critical thinkers and analysts. However, they tend to apply "what has worked in the past" and assume it will work in the current context. New methods and paradigms may threaten the Overseer's need for stability.

What You Can Contribute To the Ministry

Within a typical church, Overseers can be effective staff members, ministry leaders or deacons, but they must have clearly defined areas of responsibility, goals and objectives. Overseers will build a support team that holds strongly to the traditional values of hard work, loyalty and sacrifice.

If Overseers are not permitted to make system improvements or are forced to function within a system that does not make sense to them, they may become frustrated and develop a negative or critical attitude. Because of their expressive nature, their critical attitude may hamper the ministry.

How Leadership Can Support You

Overseers must feel that they are fully responsible for their assigned domain. They have a strong need to know where and how they "belong." Because of this, Overseers value some form of commissioning for service. This sense of empowerment is crucial to their sense of authority, responsibility and accountability.

Overseers may need help in learning to work with less traditional personality types in a healthy ministry team. It may be wise to partner a less directive and more sensitive person with an Overseer when having to address serious team member issues.

The Evangelist

Heart's Cry Statement

Let me promote what's new.

Highlights

- A promoter of self, systems and organizations
- Helpful in launching new ministry startups and team mobilization
- Helpful in cause-based fund raising campaigns
- Highly social; can adapt themselves to those around them
- Typically not strong team leaders, though they have outstanding interpersonal skills and attract people to them
- Good at multi-tasking, preferring to have many irons in the fire
- The latest cause is the greatest cause

Who God Made You to Be

By "Evangelist" we do not refer to the traditional ministry role of proclaiming Christ to others (though this personality can be outstanding in the Biblical office of evangelist if properly gifted by the Holy Spirit). The term is being used here as it is used in the secular corporate world—an Evangelist is a promoter of self, systems and organizations.

If only the Church would learn to appreciate and unleash this personality, an incredible quantity of ministries could be launched and ministry teams mobilized! God created this personality to be a natural marketer of themselves and the organizations they represent.

It is possible that Evangelists are underutilized within the Church because they appear overly busy and obsessed with materialism. They tend to have large homes, drive expensive cars, wear the latest clothes and eat at the finest restaurants. They are constantly busy. They seem to know everyone.

Ministries tend to dissociate their ministry projects with the appearance of "materialism" and so may dissociate themselves from Evangelists. This is unfortunate because God created this personality to influence the influencers of the world. The Evangelist is highly personable, mixes well with all people, and is not threatened by the world's social elite.

Ministry leaders may also seek to avoid asking such "busy" people to "do more." What many leaders fail to understand is that the Evangelist personality is the most skilled personality type at multitasking. They live and thrive on having many irons in the fire! The latest thing is always the greatest thing with an Evangelist.

What You Can Contribute To the Ministry

When a ministry seeks to develop a new program, plant a church, or build a ministry team, it would be wise to bring an Evangelist on board to spearhead the communication process. Evangelists are helpful in communicating the vision, expressing the need, building consensus, and raising funds. They may also be helpful in the startup phase of the venture.

Evangelists, however, are quite poor at management and follow-through. If an Evangelist is asked to manage a program past the startup phase, it is a set-up for failure. Ironically, even though Evangelists attract people to themselves by the strength of their relational personality, they are poor team leaders. The self-promotion aspect of this personality type is in contradiction to the self-effacing team leader who places team members before self. The Evangelist was created by God to facilitate ministry startup and promote established ministry structures.

How Leadership Can Support You

A ministry that is struggling to be effective may benefit by contracting an Evangelist as a consultant in order to seek input and guidance on how to restructure, position and promote the ministry for maximum strategic impact. Evangelists have a God-given ability to perceive how to position an organization to make a significant impact among people. Ministry leaders should be prepared for proposals that may be deemed as "risky" because Evangelists are great risk-takers. This is part of the secret to their success—and in some cases, failure. If you don't have risk, however, there is no need for faith.

The Super Leader

Heart's Cry Statement

Let me take charge of the leadership team.

Highlights

- A leader of leaders
- A primary influencer within the organization
- A strong strategic planner
- A change agent
- Significant ability to mobilize people to a vision or cause

Who God Made You to Be

The Super Leader is usually the primary influencer within the organization. The Super Leader is generally known by many within the ministry; possibly more by reputation than by personal relationship. The Super Leader mixes with other leaders and is a leader of leaders.

Super Leaders are visionary and change advocates. They are often the originators and architects of new ministry ventures and building campaigns. They tend to be excellent strategic planners. In their secular life, they are usually business owners or corporate executives and are accustomed to being in charge, setting direction and *not* being challenged.

Super Leaders see themselves as living on top of the organizational pyramid. It does not matter if this is true officially or not, because their influence has the same result. As the pinnacle of the organizational pyramid, they tend to devalue input from people under them unless requested. They value competence and proven achievement and are highly result-oriented.

Super Leaders value results over relationships, which means that more relational personalities may distrust them. Super Leaders justify "results over relationships" by arguing that far more people will benefit from their policies and systems—and they are probably correct.

Super Leaders can be blunt and intimidating. They must continually surrender this aspect of their personality to the Lordship of Jesus Christ and the sanctifying work of the Holy Spirit.

What You Can Contribute To the Ministry

The Super Leader unites and inspires other leaders to influence and impact the rest of the ministry. Whatever the Super Leader seeks to accomplish, the result is that the ministry seems to fall in line and fully support it. The Super Leader is adept at mobilizing the ministry and its ministry teams.

How Leadership Can Support You

God can do incredible things through Super Leaders—but only if they are mature in faith, Biblically sound and walking humbly before God and pastoral leadership. It is wise, therefore, to avoid putting Super Leaders into prominent leadership roles unless their lives truly reflect these qualities. Super Leaders who seek their own agenda can be devastating to a ministry; they may attempt to usurp the authority of other leaders, including the senior pastor and other pastoral staff. Their strong personalities and skillfulness, if used inappropriately, can cause church splits. Care should be taken that Super Leaders are only placed into positions of authority after they have been tested and proved themselves to be true spiritual leaders. This principle is expressly outlined in First Timothy 3 and Titus 1.

The Fraternal Leader

Heart's Cry Statement

Let me build a band of brothers and sisters.

Highlights

- Likes to invest in a group or team
- Values ideas as well as people
- Comfortable in the role of instructor or mentor
- Excellent problem-solving skills
- Ultimate goal is to always benefit people
- May become too emotionally involved in the lives of others

Who God Made You to Be

Fraternal Leaders are outgoing in nature and attract people to them. They are also sensitive to the feelings and perspectives of others and are able to facilitate an affirming and positive group dynamic. They greatly value harmonious relationships.

Fraternal Leaders prefer to process theories, concepts, and ideas rather than articulate facts. They are articulate and able to communicate effectively with their team, stimulating discussion and expression within the group. The Fraternal Leader is very comfortable in the role of instructor or mentor. Their ability to relate to people as well as ideas enables the Fraternal Leader to build a unique bond with group members.

Fraternal Leaders can also be creative problem solvers. They can tackle multiple projects at the same time and effectively lead project teams. Their satisfaction is derived from the belief that whatever project they are working on will have a positive influence or impact upon people. The Fraternal Leader is never focused on the task; rather, the task is merely a stepping stone to help people. The Fraternal Leader is very open to new ideas, programs or systems that will enable them to more effectively help people.

What You Can Contribute To the Ministry

Fraternal Leaders make excellent pastors, small group leaders and team leaders. They prefer to be responsible for their own team, cell group or congregation. This personality may most closely exemplify the nature of the ministry relationship between Jesus and His disciples.

Fraternal Leaders can very easily be viewed by their students and group attendees as their personal "mentor." If the Fraternal Leader is spiritually mature and scripturally astute, he or she may establish long-term relationships with the group members and facilitate their spiritual formation through all the steps from seeker to leader.

How Leadership Can Support You

With the popularity of the small group movement, cell church and satellite church models for dividing large ministries into manageable and relational entities, pastoral leaders should seek out Fraternal Leaders and invest considerable time and effort to equip them for healthy Biblically-based ministry.

Fraternal Leaders are prone to the danger of becoming too emotionally attached to their students. They may develop a "savior complex" in which they feel a need to carry or solve everyone's problems. This unhealthy trait can be kept in check with counseling and accountability from more senior pastoral leadership.

The Servant

Heart's Cry Statement

Let me make sure everyone has what they need to succeed.

Highlights

- People-focused
- Needs to work with people
- Tends to value social propriety and traditions
- A resource provider, making sure everyone has what they require.
- Very sensitive personality that can be easily wounded
- Can take on leadership roles effectively

Who God Made You to Be

The Servant is practically-minded and people-focused, with very high social skills and the need to be with, work with, or help people.

Without human interaction, they may become easily depressed. Servants can effectively lead teams to accomplish a social event. Banquets, parties, community fairs and bazaars are examples of the type of events they value (consider also church service programming). They tend to value social propriety and traditions. They are loyal, trustworthy and respectable.

Servants do enjoy helping people, but gain even more satisfaction by being able to resource others to ensure their success. They see themselves as a provider of necessities. They contribute to organizational leadership and its teams by ensuring that everyone has what they need to succeed. In this sense, Servants feel most satisfied when they have contributed to the benefit or success of others.

Servants are very sensitive and can be easily wounded emotionally. When they feel attacked, they may respond quite emotionally. Following the episode, they will likely internalize the relational problem, and blame themselves for the breakdown in relationship. Their resourcing nature will convince their heart and mind that if only they had better provided the other person with what they needed, then the relationship would not have deteriorated. Servants dislike conflict and will do anything in their power to bring harmony. Sometimes Servants seek relational harmony by focusing on the good and selectively ignoring the bad, resulting in unaddressed relational issues that rise to the surface in due time. Because the Servant refused to see the bad, they may be blindsided and ill-prepared when finally forced to deal with it.

What You Can Contribute To the Ministry

Servants do well in public, visible leadership roles; they are outgoing, love being with people, and communicate well. They epitomize the servant-leader model. They can be dynamic "point-people" on stage, while at the same time be caring "ministers" off stage. That is why many Servants become pastors, counselors or social workers. They have a need to be with people and invest in the welfare of others. They want to resource others spiritually and physically.

How Leadership Can Support You

Servants respond to praise and gratitude: the more they feel appreciated, the harder they serve. Superiors who demonstrate genuine appreciation by verbal and concrete means, and also display a character that the Servant respects, will likely be esteemed by the Servant.

The Protagonist

Heart's Cry Statement

Let me gather people for a social or ministry event.

Highlights

- Highly social
- All of life is "a stage"
- Needs to be in the center of any important social activity
- Has a flair for style and the arts
- Values cultural relevancy
- May "drop the ball" and not finish what was started

Who God Made You to Be

The Protagonist is highly social and needs to be in the center of any activity or event. Protagonists can be leaders or support people within a group context, but they tend to steal the show. They enjoy being in the spotlight and their vibrant personality attracts people to them. They seem to always be upbeat, enthusiastic and positive. Protagonists have a flair for style and the arts, and tend to be up on all the latest cultural trends.

Protagonists need to be with people, to express themselves and their ideas. Protagonists need to feel valued and appreciated. When in a role that violates these fundamental needs, Protagonists become depressed, or detach themselves emotionally and physically from the role, often compensating by talking too much on the phone or making many trips to the water cooler.

Protagonists are so busy relating and creating that they tend to forget the many tasks at hand. When the Protagonist does commit to a task or project, it will generally be because they perceive that the result will be of benefit to the people they will impact.

What You Can Contribute To the Ministry

Protagonists are often attracted to ministry, music, and theater—any position in which there is a gathering of people and a stage, whether figuratively or literally. Protagonists can make excellent visual point people for people-intensive projects. The Protagonist will likely be aware of what issues and communication style is relevant within the current culture. They can also lead highly dynamic relational small groups.

How Leadership Can Support You

Pastoral leaders can benefit greatly by including a Protagonist on a ministry design team; expect the Protagonist to make non-traditional recommendations. Protagonists may be able to identify and communicate a vision for ministry, but will generally have difficulty implementing the vision.

Protagonists are not good with details and follow-through, so they need to be partnered with detail-oriented people and administrators. If properly supported, however, Protagonists can generate considerable enthusiasm for new ventures and breathe new life into old programming.

It is best to empower the Protagonist to interact socially, dream creatively, and perform effectively. Let supportive team members pick up the balls the Protagonist drops.

The Creator

Heart's Cry Statement

Let me invent new and better ways to extend our ministry impact.

Highlights:

- The Thomas Edison of ministry systems
- Highly resistive to established ways of doing anything
- Attracted to innovative ministries
- Possesses strong verbal and multi-tasking abilities
- Gravitates to roles in technology, mechanics or organizational development
- Makes a great systems analyst and consultant

Who God Made You to Be

God has instilled this personality with one of His primary attributes—the ability to create new things, systems and programs.

Creators are social individuals with strong verbal and multi-tasking skills. They love to be involved in creative problem-solving and tend to gravitate to roles involving technology, custom mechanics or organizational development. They are often entrepreneurs, going "where no one has gone before." They are also excellent systems analysts and can serve effectively as systems or organizational consultants.

The Creator strongly believes in the value of his or her innovative creations, because of all the thought invested into birthing the new idea. However, if others (particularly leadership) do not respond in an affirming and enthusiastic manner, the Creator may feel dejected and either work tirelessly to make the new idea more acceptable or write off non-supporters as people who "don't get it."

Creators are "power people" and need opportunities to interact with other "power people" within the organization. They also lead teams effectively, although the team atmosphere they generate will be unstructured and highly creative—a fun and, at times, chaotic place to serve.

Creators are good at so many things that they have difficulty focusing their talent and may overextend their commitments. In particular, their family relationships may be neglected when overextended in the creative process. Creators are also quick to start a project but will usually leave the finishing to others.

What You Can Contribute To the Ministry

The Creator is particularly helpful to a ministry in fields such as church planting, satellite ministries, technology integration, multimedia, multi-track service design and new ministry development.

The Creator has an instinctive awareness of "things lacking" or "potential lost" when they observe a ministry's structures and programs. The heart cry of the Creator is likely to be: "If only." They can always envision a better and more effective way to accomplish any goal. It is not important that the new thing does not exist or has never existed because God has placed them on this planet to create new things for His glory and the benefit of His people.

How Leadership Can Support You

If more ministries valued the Creator personality instead of trying to avoid risk, the Church could accomplish much more for the kingdom of Christ. In fact, statements that infer a preference for "safe ministry" will likely turn off the Creator. If your ministry lacks Creator personalities, it is likely that the attitude and atmosphere of the ministry unconsciously communicates that Creators are not welcome.

A ministry can benefit greatly from Creators, but leaders must learn to appreciate change and help their members to do so as well. Otherwise, Creators may end up being vilified as those who changed the church others have grown to love. If this occurs, your ministry will likely lose this valuable and rare person to another ministry.

The Disseminator

Heart's Cry Statement

Let me tell you about the great things God is doing!

Highlights

- Values a mission
- Values serving with people to accomplish a mission
- Values a mission that benefits people
- Passionate, with strong relational and verbal skills
- Gifted at the startup phases of a project
- Attracts people to any new or hot activity

Who God Made You to Be

Disseminators have three passions: 1) the mission, 2) serving with people to accomplish the mission, and 3) knowing that the mission will benefit others. Disseminators are social and value the synergy of a creative team environment. They are influential individuals who often move into positions of leadership by virtue of their passion, relational skills, and communication gifts. Team members are initially attracted to the Disseminator as a team leader.

One of the key traits of Disseminators is that when they are passionate about something, everyone around them knows it. Passion pours out of Disseminators through their relational and verbal skills. When they commit to a project or mission, they may attack it so zealously that they forget to eat and sleep.

What You Can Contribute To the Ministry

Disseminators are an excellent personality type for new ministry ventures and church plants. Not only do they possess many of the entrepreneurial skills needed in the startup process, but they also approach new ventures from a perspective of how to impact and attract people rather than how to build an organization.

Disseminators can also make excellent missionaries when gifted by God with evangelistic gifts and called by Him into the role of evangelist.

Disseminators can also excel at supporting a ministry organization's communication efforts. In fact, this personality is often drawn to vocational roles such as public relations, marketing and writing. They are also attracted to visual communication media such as graphic arts, PowerPoint, and video. However, in these communication roles, the Disseminator must exist within the synergy of a team context. They cannot function in isolation.

How Leadership Can Support You

While the Disseminator is gifted at accomplishing the startup phases of a project, he or she has difficulty managing projects to a conclusion. A healthy support team with strong detail and administrative gifts will pick up the pieces and help ensure the success of the Disseminator and the mission project they so passionately believe in.

The Analyzer

Heart's Cry Statement

Let me help improve the effectiveness of our present ministries.
Highlights
• Values analyzing current ministry structures and looks for ways to improve them
• Very concerned about quality and quality improvement
• Highly dependable and conscientious
• Supports new ventures only if the risks are minimized

- Lives in the moment with extreme focus
- Tends to work alone, but can function in small teams

Who God Made You to Be

God created Analyzers to refine and improve information, systems, and structures. They value detailed and technical work. They pride themselves on conducting a thorough analysis of whatever is presented to them and adding value to the organization by correcting errors, improving efficiency, and clarifying systems to make the work of others more effective. They are the quality improvement people within an organization. Analyzers are highly dependable, very loyal to their superiors and respectful of authority structures and pecking-order within a team.

Analyzers are hard-working, quiet, and submissive. They consistently demonstrate these traits at work, within their ministry roles at church, and within their family relationships. Analyzers are highly committed to their spouse and children, heritage, and traditional roots. This does not mean that they are not open to new things. They may take the attitude that the new is good as long as risks are minimized and the old is respected.

Analyzers live in the moment with extreme focus. They may find that they so much live in the moment that, when at work they are 100 percent committed to work; when at church they are 100 percent committed to ministry; when at home, 100 percent committed to their spouse and children. The result is that Analyzers try to systematize and compartmentalize their duties and commitments. Compartmentalization inevitably results in a collision of duties and commitments. Because Analyzers tend to be ardent people-pleasers, they may find the collision of their various duties very stressful; after all, they never want to let anyone down! To compensate they may forego sleep and food until their responsibilities are accomplished. Analyzers tend to resist delegating duties to others, believing that no one can accomplish the task as well as they can. Their past attempts at delegating duties may have been less than successful.

Relationally, Analyzers are non-confrontational, quiet and respectable. They tend to be responsive to the relational overtures of others and are less likely to take the initiative to make a first contact. However, once a connection has been initiated by another, the Analyzer will be viewed as warm, personable and intelligent. Because Analyzers are relational responders rather than initiators, they can be seen as cool, aloof, distant or stuck-up—an unfortunate misreading of this personality. In fact, Analyzers can be quite compassionate and patient with people, especially the emotionally needy or mentally challenged.

What You Can Contribute To the Ministry

Analyzers want to see continual improvement in the ministry and they are willing to work hard to make it so. Whatever program or ministry they are responsible for will run smoothly and trouble-free. Because they think in terms of systems and structures, Analyzers function best within the constraints of an established program structure. Non-programmed roles could include content management, written communications, administrative duties and bookkeeping. Since Analyzers are drawn to the technical, they may also make good managers of the ministry website.

How Leadership Can Support You

Analyzers can become overly involved in supporting others because they tend to focus 100 % on the moment. Ministry leaders need to help keep Analyzers from over-committing. They require help in learning to prioritize and say "no" to opportunities that may detract from their true personal, vocational and ministerial priorities.

The Artisan

Heart's Cry Statement

What can I build to help our ministry?

Highlights

- Uses his or her hands to create, build or heal
- May be a tradesman or a professional in the medical industry
- Aspires to be a virtuoso in his or her area of expertise
- Values concrete results, not abstract ideas
- Receives enjoyment through the service process
- Devalues schedules and systems

Who God Made You to Be

Artisans are single-minded in their approach to life. They utilize their skills of observation and mastery of tools to create, build or heal. Examples of roles that contain many Artisans include: surgeon, computer programmer, carpenter, plumber or metal worker. Artisans must utilize their hands. They feel that creating with their hands is play. After a long day at work, they may return home only to spend the evening using their hands to create.

Artisans are the least verbal of all personality types, taking the attitude that actions and accomplishments "speak for themselves." They dislike formalized education. Pen, paper and books are simply far too abstract for them. They value concrete results. It is not likely that Artisans will attend a Bible study sponsored by the local church or serve as classroom teachers. Education, philosophy and theology are not highly esteemed by them. Artisans prefer practical application to passive study.

Whether professionals or tradesmen, Artisans have one major thing in common: They seek to become virtuosos in their area of specialty. They are highly proficient experts in their field, and they take considerable pride in their ability. Even though they may appreciate comments of gratitude and admiration for the service they provide, they judge for themselves the quality of their own work. Personal satisfaction is achieved through the service process and knowing that they have done the very best job possible.

Artisans work alone or in small groups of like-skilled artisans whom they respect. Similarly, they are attracted to recreational opportunities that offer solitude. They often enjoy activities such as hunting, fishing or sewing. Some Artisans may pursue extreme sports such as skiing or rock climbing, but they are activities that can be enjoyed alone or in small groups of like-skilled and respected individuals.

What You Can Contribute To the Ministry

The Artisan will generally serve in ministry by providing handcrafted services. They will build stage sets, participate in construction projects, serve in short-term mission ventures to build an orphanage, or develop software for the ministry. Surgeons or dentists will likely participate in short-term missions to use their medical skills while providing *probono* or discount services.

How Leadership Can Support You

Artisans do not value schedules, procedures or authority structures. They want to conduct their craft when, where and how they choose. To expect an Artisan to be punctual to a meeting is likely fruitless. Artisans are more likely to contribute if they are allowed to flex an established schedule to make it fit their personal and family time.

The Planner

Heart's Cry Statement

Let me create an effective and innovative strategic plan and help it become a reality.

Highlights

- Excels at strategic planning
- Sees all the steps necessary to accomplish any project
- Is proficient at managing projects through all stages of development
- Prefers science, technology and organizational philosophy
- Has very demanding expectations
- Is stimulated by vision and will pursue a vision relentlessly to its conclusion
- Are strong strategic leaders and consultants

Who God Made You to Be

Planners excel at strategic planning regardless of the size of a project. They have a God-given ability to visualize all the steps that need to be accomplished in order to successfully conclude a venture. Planners apply logical and technical systems. They can quickly size up and organize an abstract idea and devise a solid system that will provide positive results. Because of this ability, they often serve as corporate executives, business owners and technology designers.

Planners are virtually tireless in their obsession to create innovative and original solutions to problems. Originality is a very important attribute of their personality—they are at their best when given a challenge that currently has no known solution. They are very adept at observing such opportunities for innovation and leading the team to create the product, service or organization that will address the observed need.

While Planners develop systems and solutions that must have a practical application, their mind spins in the world of operational philosophy. Better than any other personality, Planners excel at taking an abstract idea and developing a practical solution. Although the Planner does invent, he or she is not satisfied until the invention has been properly designed, developed, completed and generally accepted. It is the ability to lead throughout the stages of any large and innovative project that makes the Planner so unique.

The Planner is typically an intellectual, often with almost genius capabilities, and is well-versed on many topics, but leans toward science, technology and organizational philosophy.

Planners are relentless in their pursuit of a vision. They are often found working long hours, even to the point of neglecting food and sleep. In fact, Planners may often have difficulty sleeping because their minds are constantly in motion. They cannot help but analyze the information of the day, envision possibilities for the future and construct innovative systems.

Planners tend to work alone much of the time but value having a highly skilled team to lead. The Planner must have a high regard for the professionalism and skill of each team member. The demanding nature and high standards held by Planners may make the people around them feel inadequate. The Planner builds team commitment by selling the virtue of the system, product or organization to the team members.

What You Can Contribute To the Ministry

Planners are very helpful in guiding ministry leaders through strategic planning, designing new structures and leading a church plant or developing a satellite ministry. Planners also make excellent teachers, consultants, leadership equippers and software developers.

How Leadership Can Support You

Ministries may have difficulty identifying Planners because they are the rarest of all personality types. Many ministries seek to apply proven models and do not value innovation. But by their very nature, Planners do not fit well in the establishment.

When Planners are empowered for a task, they may envision and speak about the future of the project as though it is already a reality—and to them it is! Leadership, in such cases, will need to work hard to catch up to the Planner. If leadership does not make this effort, they will either default to "followership" or reject the work of the Planner (and thereby the Planner him/herself) as too complex.

The Guide

Heart's Cry Statement

Let me help people grow spiritually.

Highlights

- Gifted counselor and mentor
- Highly people-focused
- Prefers one-on-one or small-group relationships
- Typically works behind the scenes
- Has significant influence on the individuals he or she serves
- A common pastoral personality

Who God Made You to Be

Guides are gifted counselors and mentors. They have a need for innovative problem-solving but are focused on people instead of systems. They want to help people grow both emotionally and spiritually through their development struggles. Guides may find that they play this role, perhaps informally, within their interpersonal relationships. People who require a little extra support and grace are attracted to them. Guides value a few deep relationships rather than many social contacts.

Guides are highly sensitive individuals who often have insight into why people behave as they do, even if the other person is oblivious to their behavioral motivations. This insight may be a natural personality trait, but is generally strengthened through considerable study in the humanities and psychology.

Typically, Guides are not leaders in the visible sense, nor are they leaders of groups, although they can function within a group context. But if leadership is defined as "influence," then Guides exhibit considerable influence through their authentic and close relationships.

While Guides can easily gain insight into what makes others tick, the reverse is seldom true. It is difficult to become acquainted with them because Guides are intellectually and emotionally complex people and have a quiet nature.

Guides are unassuming individuals. Their work and ministry may never be visible and will likely never be celebrated publicly. Yet, as the Bible teaches, God places a special honor upon those parts of the Body of Christ that are less obvious.

What You Can Contribute To the Ministry

Guides often enter the ministry as small-church pastors or pastoral counselors. They benefit a ministry through their counseling and mentorship skills in one-on-one sessions with individuals. They can also help develop recovery and restoration ministries, providing support and training for other counselors and group facilitators.

As lay people, Guides can provide a good barometer for pastoral leadership because they will be keenly aware of the "feelings" of the congregation. They see themselves as highly empathetic and have strong listening skills.

How Leadership Can Support You

Guides need their own "flock" to shepherd. Leadership may consider assigning a small group, or better yet, permit the Guide to be a spiritual formation mentor for as many individuals as they can support. Leadership should also understand that the Guides are used to giving others support, but may have difficulty receiving support from others—even if they need it.

The Minister

Heart's Cry Statement

Let me protect God's people from harm.

Highlights

- A shepherding person that values protecting people
- Avoids risks if at all possible
- Leads small groups and individuals well
- Functions well only in small organizational structures
- A modest and humble individual
- Values heritage and tradition

Who God Made You to Be

Ministers are what the name implies: pastoral people who invest their lives in the welfare of others. Their self-sacrificing nature enables them to place the needs of others before their own. Ministers want to guard, guide and protect the people they care about. They are deeply committed to their family and are highly loyal in their relational commitments. Ministers are not showy individuals. They are usually happy with a modest home, a used car and department store clothing.

Ministers are likely to be soft-spoken, warm and humble people who prefer one-on-one relationships. They can have a firm and cool demeanor when viewed from a distance, but they are not as they may appear. They simply take their role to care for others seriously. They are serious but not aloof. They view themselves as paternal (or maternal, as the case may be) when in close relationships with others. In keeping with their sense of protectionism, Ministers are respectful of authority and those that possess significant titles.

Ministers are NOT risk-takers. They fear that taking a risk might mean that someone could get hurt. They are detail-oriented and accurately handle facts and information. In fact, they may pride themselves on their ability to memorize and recall facts, information and illustrations from the past and use them to apply to the immediate context.

What You Can Contribute To the Ministry

Ministers are valuable support assets. They serve well as pastoral care or visitation pastors and make excellent one-on-one mentors. They also make excellent small group leaders, serving well as counselors and leaders within restoration and recovery ministries.

How Leadership Can Support You

Because of their protective nature, Ministers who are placed in positions of leadership may stunt the growth of the organization, so that it does not realize its full potential. This is true for two primary reasons:

1.   The Minister cannot personally care for every individual in a larger organization. The desire to care for everyone may cause the Minister to subconsciously limit the growth of the organization to a size that is manageable.

2.   The Minister probably will not take the risks required to grow an organization through its various stages of development. The Minister thinks in terms of one-on-one relationships instead of organizations or systems.

This does not mean that an organization should replace the Minister with someone better suited for organizational growth; but the Minister may not be best suited to "run" the organization. Furthermore, to develop an organization for maximum impact, the Minister needs to value and trust the leaders that excel in the abilities the Minister does not possess. Just because a Minister may not be able to serve everyone in the organization (and he or she may feel a responsibility to do so) does not mean that people will not be cared for in the ministry. There are other adequate systems and people available to accomplish this task.

The Adjutant

Heart's Cry Statement

Let me support tangible projects that help others by working hard behind the scenes, addressing issues that require an attention to detail and accuracy.

Highlights

- Seeks to excel in his or her area of responsibility, preferring to support people or projects that require a level of accuracy and detail
- Highly focused; does not normally excel at multitasking
- Requires an atmosphere that is free of conflict and interruption
- Prefers to work one-on-one with others rather than in groups
- Can be highly empathetic and compassionate, especially in crisis situations
- Prefers to work behind the scenes and avoids public presentations

Who God Made You to Be

Adjutants aspire to excel in their areas of responsibility, preferring the detailed aspects related to people or projects. The Adjutant can be seen in such roles as artist, counselor, computer programmer, social worker, administrative assistant and nurse. While these sample roles may at first appear quite divergent, they possess common themes that require the Adjutant to exhibit focused attention to detail, an empathetic and compassionate spirit and a desire to play a supportive role in relationships and projects.

Their personality is a unique combination of a deep internalized world, a desire to focus on details and reality, make decisions according to their personal values and refrain from structures and rules they perceive as "restrictive." Adjutants are typically gentle-spirited, kindhearted, self-sacrificing and loyal.

What You Can Contribute To the Ministry

Adjutants prefer to play a supportive behind-the-scenes role in any project, yet they need to feel valued and recognized for their contributions. They are sensitive to the feelings and needs of others and will likely not assert themselves if they feel that doing so may offend or hurt another individual. They are often perceived as quiet and unassuming, yet they can exhibit considerable warmth and compassion.

Adjutants have little desire to control or dominate people or projects and do not typically display a stubborn spirit regarding rules, methods or procedures. In fact, they commonly consider themselves to be flexible and adaptable.

Strategic planning and long-term vision and goals are not often appealing to the Adjutant. They perceive the present need and would prefer to stay focused upon the issue at hand. Their "serve-in-the-moment" passion allows them to excel in support-intensive and crisis management roles.

The Adjutant, by definition, is not a leader and will typically resist pressure to assume a leadership position. Do not ask an Adjutant to cast vision, plan a project, or lead a project team. However, he or she will likely excel as a small group leader primarily responsible for the emotional and spiritual welfare of a few individuals. The Adjutant will also likely excel in supportive roles that involve one-on-one mentorship or counseling. He or she may also enjoy visitation ministry—reaching out to those in hospitals, nursing homes and shut-ins.

Regarding the "business" of ministry, the Adjutant may excel in such roles as administrative assistants, deacons, bookkeepers, database managers, resource center managers, food pantry managers, etc. The compassionate and supportive nature of Adjutants may also lead them to take a strong interest in local and global missions where they may serve the needs of others in ways that are practical and immediate.

Adjutants can, at times, display a strong artistic ability. They are deep thinkers and feelers, and this aspect of their personality may express itself through art, music, drama and poetry.

How Leadership Can Support You

Adjutants may require coaxing from leaders to get them to share their opinions and perspectives. Don't accept such statements as "I don't know," or "Whatever you think is best." The thoughts, feelings and perspectives of the Adjutant are valid and should be sought after and respected. The Adjutant is far more sensitive to the feelings and needs of others than most leader-type personalities, and leaders would do well to allow the Adjutants in their lives to be a "window" into the emotional state of their congregation or ministry team.

The Adjutant desires to help leaders succeed and plays an essential support role. Most leaders find the services of the Adjutant to be indispensable. Leaders need to remember to affirm the Adjutants in their life and to give them their due credit (and the leader's gratitude) for the services they have rendered. Failure to provide this necessary feedback may lead the Adjutant to feel devalued and de-motivated; ultimately the Adjutant may resign his or her position.

The Designer

Heart's Cry Statement

Let me create a blueprint for new ministry development.

Highlights

- Creates a blueprint of system or organizational design
- Works independently
- Turns chaos into structures to be implemented by others
- Has a small relational pool since relationships are viewed as "hard work"
- Can observe and address poor logic in a system design
- May require support in dealing with difficult interpersonal relationships

Who God Made You to Be

Designers like to take chaos and mold it like clay to construct highly logical and applicable systems and structures. They focus on one task at a time and will invest long hours learning all they can about the ideas, concepts and philosophies that impact their current project. Then they seek to provide a framework to make these abstractions usable in a concrete fashion.

Designers are quiet, introspective people. They are highly intelligent. They tend to view the world as "projects" to be accomplished. They want to add order and structure to their world and feel satisfied when that goal is achieved project by project. Designers tend to believe their work is accomplished once a plan has been created. Implementation and application are the responsibilities of others.

Designers tend to be poor relationship managers. They are so focused on the task at hand and devising structure and system designs that they have little energy left for the "hard work" of maintaining relationships. Their relational pool is small. They generally work alone and behind the scenes. Although they can work in small teams comprised of people whom they respect, they quickly feel "drained" by too much relational contact.

What You Can Contribute To the Ministry

Designers are rare and may be absent in many ministries. However, they can benefit a ministry if called upon to develop a plan on paper in the early phases of new ministry development. This blueprint will help keep all personalities related to the project on task and unified. Designers will also be able to observe and address any poor logic or issues associated with the project that have not been thoroughly addressed by the ministry leaders.

How Leadership Can Support You

If possible, it may be beneficial to bring on board a Planner personality to help the Designer understand the philosophy that undergirds the new ministry venture. The Designer will be able to take the strategic steps envisioned by the Planner and articulate those steps on paper in a logical and concise manner.

The Reconciler

Heart's Cry Statement

Let me heal broken relationships, between people and between God and His people.

Highlights

- Relates strongly to the concepts of "guilt" and "grace"
- Highly relational
- Seeks to reconcile people with people as well as people with God
- Commonly serves on the mission field or in mission and counseling organizations
- May be intolerant of his or her own failures
- Needs to be affirmed for who he or she is, not simply for the task performed

Who God Made You to Be

Reconcilers identify well with the Apostle Paul's tension between our guilt and God's grace. Reconcilers are grace-givers and seek emotional and spiritual harmony and unity with individuals and in interpersonal relationships. However, they are often hypersensitive to sin in themselves and in others. While Reconcilers are gracious in helping others address and overcome personal sin, they can be far less gracious with themselves. They may "beat themselves up" emotionally for their "failures" and struggle with feelings of acceptance by God and His people. They may struggle with issues of self-worth and their place in this world as they wrestle with a sense of guilt. They may feel that they must perform "good deeds" to compensate for their failures.

Reconcilers like to work with people rather than ideas or tasks. They prefer a few in-depth relationships rather than many social contacts. They work alone well and can be frustrated if interrupted too often. When communicating, Reconcilers may illustrate points using word pictures, analogies and metaphors.

What You Can Contribute To the Ministry

Reconcilers are very receptive to personal involvement in causes that make a difference. This personality type would most likely respond to a missionary's appeal to come join in the work they are doing in Africa or the Muslim world. Reconcilers want to make a difference and heal broken relationships. The combination of these two passions enables them to fit well in such roles as pastor, missionary, counselor, city mission director, restoration and recovery ministry support staff and cross-cultural minister. They may also serve well as small group leaders.

How Leadership Can Support You

It is important that pastors affirm and support the Reconciler in clear and consistent ways. The Reconciler needs to know that *what* they are doing and, more importantly, who they are personally is important, valued and appreciated. To help the Reconciler be effective in their ministry, leaders should pour upon them blessings of grace. Leaders should emphasize the value of the Reconciler, not for what he or she has accomplished, but for who they are in Christ Jesus.

Leadership should observe carefully whether a Reconciler is being too sacrificial or working too much. While this workaholic mentality may benefit the ministry, it is also likely a sign of spiritual illness. The Reconciler's sense of personal guilt may drive him or her into a works-relationship with God and others, rather than trust in God's gift of grace. Leadership should consider providing accountability relationships to help the Reconciler stay on a healthy spiritual path.

Leadership Style Reports

The following reports are also available the Leadership Style assessment offered by AssessMe.org. Condensed versions of these reports are available through the Leadership Style assessment offered by E-Church Essentials.

The Pioneering Leader

Highlights

- Entrepreneurial; needs to be involved leading new ministry development
- Highly motivated by a noble vision and driven to make the vision a reality
- Very task-oriented, but views tasks as steps in a grand mission that will bless others
- Brings to the team vision, direction, passion and motivation
- Values high-risk/high-reward ministry; is likely to be a dominant agent of change

Report

Pioneering Leaders are willing to push themselves and take appropriate risks, striving to discover and reach long-term goals, "forgetting what is behind, and straining for what lies ahead" (Phil. 3:12). They are passionate and wholly committed to a vision. Paul is a great example of a leader who was focused on pushing out the boundaries of the church despite the personal risk.

Pioneering Leaders are at their strongest in the early stages of a vision or project; they enjoy seeking out where God is calling. As time passes, however they may lose interest in the implementation of a vision, eagerly looking ahead to the next challenge. Pioneers are very entrepreneurial; they must be involved in new ministry development. They may also excel in areas of strategic planning, administration or team leadership, but if asked to serve in such roles without being able to develop new and better methods, they will likely become frustrated.

Pioneers are very task-oriented. They typically say that they care deeply about people—and will likely cite their passion to reach others for Christ as their justification for developing new ministry systems, programs and organizations. Because they are naturally vision- and task-oriented, they may unfortunately be seen as "pushy" or insensitive—and are typically unaware that they project this impression.

Pioneers are motivated by the noble nature of the vision and the excitement of creating something new and better, and may assume everyone shares their motivation. Actually most people are not risk takers like the Pioneer but are motivated instead by stability and security. The values of the Pioneer threaten those who prefer to move slowly when changing the status quo. When those who value slow incremental change are dictating the pace of an entrepreneurial venture, they try to rein in the Pioneer, with typically devastating consequences to both the people and the project. The Pioneer must be empowered to lead. Appropriate support and accountability structures for the Pioneer should be built into the team dynamics of the Pioneer's team.

In a team context Pioneers bring vision, direction, passion and motivation to the team. They should be given full responsibility for leading and implementing the various tasks associated with the project. Since Pioneers are unique in their ability to grasp a vision, they may find themselves speaking of the future as though it already exists. For them, it does. Pioneers can already sense and feel what it will be like when the new program, system or organization is fully established.

This unique ability to "live in the future" may frustrate team members who can only see the present, and they may accuse the Pioneer of being a "dreamer." These team members see all the obstacles that must be overcome in the present and may feel overwhelmed by the enormity of it all. Pioneers are not blind to obstacles, but they are able to envision their way through obstacles in ways that others cannot.

A negative consequence of this special insight can be that the Pioneer may not adequately recognize and deal with the emotional, conceptual and practical needs of other team members. They may feel that the Pioneer disregards their concerns and devalues their role. The Pioneer, on the other hand, becomes more and more frustrated with every objection the team members raise, and will more forcefully appeal to the vision. The Pioneer may begin to feel that other team members lack the commitment and faith to complete the mission.

Because of the relational challenges in a team environment, Pioneers should have responsibility over the *tasks* of a project, while the *human* elements should be addressed by a Team Leader. Similarly, the Pioneer prefers the "big picture" and may become frustrated with the fine details of a task. Operational details should be addressed by an Administrator. Many Pioneers are excellent strategists and can create elaborate road maps to help Administrators and Team Leaders fulfill their duties. However, some Pioneers may lack this skill, and in that case a Strategic Planner should be added to the team.

Developing new systems, programs and organizations are high-risk ventures which can also involve high stress, especially months down the road of a long-term project. The Pioneer is generally ill-equipped to nurture and encourage the team through stress, so every entrepreneurial team should have a Pastor or Encourager to serve the team members emotionally, spiritually and relationally.

Pioneering Leaders need to realize that they cannot do it alone—they need the other members of their team, and the other team members need the Pioneer. First Corinthians 12 affirms that the Body of Christ has many different members who all need one another and that God positions these members just as He has determined. God creates Pioneers and positions them strategically to create new ministries, systems and organizations that will propel the kingdom of Christ forward to a world that desperately needs to know the power and love of their Creator God.

The Strategic Leader

Highlights

- A strategic planner who designs the architecture of significant ministry ventures
- May be less involved once the plan is completed, other than general oversight
- Very task-oriented; values reasonable, logical ministry systems and structures
- Brings to the team a plan for organization, role definitions and project timelines
- Brings order and structure, transforming dreams into vision and vision into manageable, practical steps

Report

Leaders who can break down visions and large aims into manageable chunks are vital to the church. Strategic Leaders have the insight and focus to work out ways to achieve the vision and can persuade others to accept their plan. When Nehemiah led the Jews in rebuilding the walls of Jerusalem, he demonstrated great strategic leadership in delegating the work. The result was that the walls were rebuilt in 52 days.

Strategic Leaders bring common sense to difficult tasks and help people see how the seemingly impossible can be achieved. They are at their strongest in the early stages of a vision or project when the "dream" needs to be delineated into a plan. Strategic Leaders are systems architects who design the road map for accomplishing the vision. But just as an architect designs a building but does not wield a hammer to build it, they may have a limited role once the strategy has been defined.

Strategic Leaders can capture the vision of the Pioneering Leader and convey a strategy for accomplishing the vision within a detailed written plan. Similarly, they can capture the detail needs of an Administrative Leader and produce a detailed plan for systems refinement. Strategic Leaders are as comfortable working with entrepreneurial projects as they are refining established programs, systems or organizations. While the Strategic Leader may also have some level of skill as an entrepreneur, administrator or team leader, it is the planning and design aspects of any project that the Strategic Leader will most value. The Strategic Leader will likely receive the greatest personal satisfaction when he or she is able to observe how their strategies have enabled other people to serve Christ more efficiently and effectively.

Strategic Leaders are very task-oriented. They typically say that they care deeply about people—and will likely cite their passion to help ministry systems to function more effectively as justification. Because they are naturally task-oriented, however, they may be seen by others as controlling and lacking in sensitivity—and they are usually unaware that they project this impression. After all, to them, their plan is a work of art. They are convinced that if their plans are implemented properly, everyone will benefit in the end.

When people do not affirm their plans, Strategic Leaders may become confused. Assuming that they must have missed some valuable information, they will typically conduct more research and rework their plan in an effort to gain wider acceptance. Ultimately, if the plan is rejected, Strategic Leaders may either take it as a personal affront or self-righteously assume that the decision makers are too stupid to understand. In reality the plan is often so detailed and intricate that it appears overwhelming to the average person.

Strategic Leaders can increase their success by presenting their plans in a manner which considers differing personality types and their various ways of processing information. Strategic Leaders should share information on a "need-to-know" basis—in other words, share only those details of the plan that their audience needs to understand it conceptually and see its relevance to them. Such restraint is difficult for many Strategic Leaders because they can easily become enamored by the complexity of the details. In their passion, they want others to appreciate all they have created. Unfortunately, only a limited number of people can truly grasp the entirety of any strategic plan.

In a team context the Strategic Leader brings to the table organizational plans, role definitions and project timelines. The Strategic Leader should be in charge of designing the architecture for project implementation. Once the road map to success has been defined, and the team member understand their roles and responsibilities, the Strategic Leader may be more comfortable handing the reins to the Pioneering Leader in an entrepreneurial venture, or the Administrative Leader or Team Leader in an ongoing project.

Because of the relational challenges of a team environment, Strategic Leaders should have responsibility over the task elements of a project, while the human elements should be addressed by a Team Leader. Similarly, because Strategic Leaders typically prefer the planning stages of a project, they may be frustrated by the practical implementation of the more mundane, ongoing tasks. Implementation details should be addressed by an Administrative Leader. The Strategic Leader is also generally ill-equipped to counsel and encourage the team for any extended period of time.

Strategic Leaders need to realize that they cannot do it alone—they need the other members of their team, and the other team members need the Strategic Leader. First Corinthians 12 affirms that the Body of Christ has many different members who all need one another and that God positions these members just as He has determined. God creates Strategic Leaders and positions them strategically to design ministry systems that will propel the kingdom of Christ forward to a world that desperately needs to know the power and love of the God who Himself designed this world.

The Administrative Leader

Highlights

- Addresses the detailed operational tasks associated with a project
- Motivated by providing resources and support to leadership in accomplishing tasks
- May struggle with multi-tasking; prefers to work from a checklist
- Brings to the team an eye for practical and administrative details
- Highly dependable and conscientious project-support team member

Appendix C   *267*

Report

Every ministry requires good stewards and managers, people with gifts of administration (Acts 6)—those who are able to plan, solve problems, delegate and organize. Without this gift the best plans go awry. The apostles delegated the practical tasks of sharing food and taking care of the widows to those gifted with the necessary skills, including Stephen and Philip.

Administrative Leaders are 100% committed to addressing the practical operational issues of any task. They are able to organize and follow through on all the necessary tasks and activities to ensure that projects are completed on time. They may struggle to relate to visionary leaders, not because they are unable to appreciate a vision, but because all they can see are the overwhelming number of practical details that must be accomplished. Administrative Leaders are often under-appreciated, having a leadership style which is less "up-front" than some of the other styles. However, much of the work simply would not get done without them.

Administrative Leaders are highly skilled at handling the details associated with any project. They like to help others be successful. In fact, they may see themselves as "the power behind the throne." They are at their strongest addressing the ongoing operational management of a project; they are practical and detail-oriented. The Administrative Leader can successfully serve an organization or a project for an extended period of time.

Administrative Leaders put the plans of Strategic Leaders into action, providing the accountability needed to make sure each task is done, and done right. They are a practical bridge between the ideal plans of the Strategic Leader and the people-oriented tasks of the Team Leader. Administrative Leaders are generally not comfortable in entrepreneurial roles. While they may have some of the skills of a Strategic Leader or Team Leader, they are most comfortable managing ongoing projects and the practical operational details of an organization.

Multi-tasking, however, is not typical among Administrative Leaders. They are people of incredible focus who tend to work their way logically down a list of responsibilities. They usually receive the greatest personal satisfaction when they can see how they have helped others be successful, and how many duties they have checked off their "to-do" list.

Administrative Leaders are very task-oriented. They typically say that they care deeply about people—and will likely cite the many things they have done to empower people to do the work of ministry. However, because they are naturally task- and detailed-oriented, they may be seen by others as very professional, but cold and aloof—and they are usually unaware that they project this impression. After all, from their perspective, they are simply trying to help others be successful! They are convinced that if people accept their practical support, everyone will benefit in the end.

When people do not affirm their supportive efforts, Administrative Leaders may respond with confusion and an overwhelming sense of failure. Assuming that they missed some valuable information, they will conduct more research in an effort to gain wider acceptance. Ultimately, if their support is rejected, Administrative Leaders may feel that they have failed their leaders and subordinates. They tend toward one of two extreme reactions: 1) They redouble their efforts, working tirelessly and sacrificially to support their superiors and subordinates, or 2) they become disillusioned, and seek to distance themselves from their perceived failure. Either extreme is unhealthy for the Administrative Leader as well as for the people he or she serves.

An inner sense of responsibility to the people they serve and the projects they support is both a blessing and a curse for Administrative Leaders. They are motivated to work tirelessly to ensure the success of others and their projects and can be a great asset to the work. However, their sense of responsibility may be so intense that they sacrifice their family, personal life and spiritual life in the process. They may also blame themselves for their perceived failures—real or imagined—for years to come.

In a team context the Administrative Leader brings to the table an eye for the details of accomplishing a project or running an organization. The Administrative Leader should be in charge of supporting the implementation of task-oriented details. Once the road map to success has been defined by a Strategic Leader, the Administrative Leader makes sure the details are completed according to designated timelines.

Administrative Leaders are not risk-takers, so it is natural for them to support Pioneering and Strategic Leaders. They are so focused on the details, that while they may be inspired by a vision, their motivation is in helping make the vision a practical reality.

Because of the relational challenges of a team environment, Administrative Leaders should have responsibility over the tasks and details of a project, while the human elements should be addressed by a Team Leader. While they may have some people-management skills, Administrative Leaders find that managing data and tasks is far easier than managing people, and they should be protected from the stress of relational conflict. The Administrative Leader is ill-equipped to counsel and encourage the team for any extended period of time, so the team should include a member who can nurture other team members emotionally, spiritually and relationally.

Administrative Leaders need to realize that they cannot do it alone—they need the other members of their team, and the other team members need the Administrative Leader. First Corinthians 12 affirms that the Body of Christ has many different members who all need one another, and that God positions these members just as He has determined. God creates Administrative Leaders and positions them strategically to support ministry systems and provide resources for those who do the work of ministry. The support of the Administrative Leader will propel the kingdom of Christ forward to a world that desperately needs to know the power and love of the God who Himself supports those who call on Him to accomplish His will and purposes in this world.

The Team Leader

Highlights

- An influencer of people, particularly within ministry team structures
- Able to perceive and value a vision and appreciate the tasks at hand to accomplish the vision, while demonstrating emotional and spiritual support for the team members
- Quickly earns the trust and allegiance of team members

- Brings motivation and affirmation to the team leadership
- If pride takes root, can be very dangerous to the unity and organizational integrity of the ministry

Report

Team Leaders influence groups, whether they have a formal leadership role or not. For the church as "the body" (1 Cor. 12) working together is clearly important. The key strengths of Team Leaders are a desire to work with others and an ability to trust them.

Healthy Team Leaders generally exhibit humility and a servant spirit—their sole aim is that the team achieves its goals. What they as individuals achieve is secondary. The greatest contribution Silas made to the church was probably training and equipping Paul, who then went on to achieve greater things.

Team Leaders are invaluable. If the church is truly to function as a body, Team Leaders are needed to ensure harmony and effectiveness in the way the team works. Team Leaders are the glue between those who implement and complete the mission and those who resource and support the team. Effective Team Leaders are able to strike a unique balance between promoting the mission objectives and communicating to team members their crucial importance—to the mission and apart from the mission.

Team Leaders are able to really listen to their team members and "hear their hearts," affirming their feelings, their perspectives and their identity in Christ. This unique ability to listen and affirm enables the Team Leader to quickly earn the trust and allegiance of team members, which can help the team become highly effective and serve for extended periods of time with limited stress or conflict.

However, the Team Leader, more than any other leadership category, has great potential for doing significant damage to a ministry organization. Because of the unique influence of Team Leaders, they are in danger of causing church splits. As skilled as they may be at pulling a cohesive team together, they can also rip an organization apart. This is usually a result of pride, working in concert with a lack of accountability.

It's not hard to see how Team Leaders can become prideful. Their ability to empower the team to accomplish significant things and their affirmation and support of each member breeds a mutual respect and love which often inspires words of high praise from team members. The more praise they receive, the easier it becomes for Team Leaders to lose sight of their spiritual poverty before God. The seed of pride begins to grow, and if not pruned back through healthy accountability and repentance, it soon gives life to arrogance. This can lead to disrespect for those in authority over the Team Leader. *After all,* the prideful Team Leader may rationalize, *look at all I and my teams have accomplished for this ministry!*

As pride and arrogance grow, the Team Leader may begin to desire greater influence and feel that if he or she had free reign, the ministry would be far more effective. In the end, if these prideful attitudes are not properly addressed, the Team Leader may attempt a takeover of the church or lead a breakaway group to start their own church.

This negative scenario can be avoided with true accountability between the ministry leadership and the Team Leader. However, ministry leaders often reward successful Team Leaders by giving them greater levels of influence over the entire ministry—yet without a corresponding greater level of practical and spiritual accountability. Giving Team Leaders "free reign" may also give "free reign" to the sin of pride.

Team Leaders are both task- and people-oriented. They typically say that they care deeply about people—and will likely cite how they have empowered people to do the work of ministry as well as specific stories of life transformation from their team members. Team Leaders are typically viewed as being warm, inspiring, considerate and motivational. Team Leaders are usually aware of how other people feel about them, for they are in tune with the feelings of others. Since their passion is to help others be successful in ministry, they are convinced that if people follow their direction and oversight everyone will benefit in the end.

When people do not affirm their leadership efforts, Team Leaders may respond by trying to understand their critics and meet their needs. In so doing, Team Leaders earn people's trust and allegiance over time. If those in authority do not affirm their leadership, Team Leaders may become embittered and seek affirmation from team members closest to them—a dangerous and potentially divisive step which may reveal their immaturity and pride.

In a team context the Team Leader brings to the table leadership, motivation and affirmation. The Team Leader should be in charge of supporting the team members who are completing a project or running the organization. Team Leaders are likely to require resources and support from an Administrative Leader since they prefer to spend their time with people rather than detailed administrative tasks.

They may, however find it difficult to be answerable to "administrative-types"; as the ones "in the trenches," they may think they know best how to do the work of ministry. Such an attitude may be a sign that pride has taken root and appropriate accountability measures should be taken. On the other hand, leadership should listen carefully to the perspectives of the Team Leader since they indeed are "in the trenches" and are best in touch with the team members' feelings and needs.

Because of the relational challenges of a team environment, Team Leaders should have responsibility over the team members and the practical implementation of a project. While they may have some administrative skills, Team Leaders find managing data and tasks far less fulfilling than managing people, and they should be protected from the stress of relational isolation in an office.

The Team Leader is usually well-equipped to counsel and encourage the team. An effective Team Leader will not only help team members accomplish a noble task, but also help them feel supported emotionally, spiritually and relationally in the process.

Team Leaders need to realize that they cannot do it alone—they need the other members of their team, and the other team members need the Team Leader. First Corinthians 12 affirms that the Body of Christ has many different members who all need one another, and that God positions these members just as He has determined. God creates Team Leaders and positions them strategically to empower people to accomplish the work of ministry. The support of the Team Leader will propel the kingdom of Christ forward to a world that desperately needs to know the power and love of the God who sent His Spirit to empower, support and guide God's people in their calling.

The Pastoral Leader

Highlights

- A real "people person"
- Prefers face-to-face human interaction and influencing people through interpersonal relationships
- Characterized as warm, tender-hearted, sincere, kind, gentle and compassionate
- Brings to the team the nurture and support that each member requires in order to persevere
- Avoids task-oriented leadership roles and extended periods in the office addressing administrative duties

Report

Many church leaders feel they ought to be Pastoral Leaders even though it is not their primary leadership style. Pastoral Leaders are real "people people" who have an important role in supporting the Pioneering Leaders, Strategic Leaders, Team Leaders and the rest of the church, particularly when times are hard. Fulfilling the vision seems less important to Pastoral Leaders. They care deeply about each individual and his or her personal and spiritual welfare. The Apostle John was a Pastoral Leader. He repeatedly calls the Body of Christ to "love one another"—a complete contrast to Paul's energetic church planting and exhortation.

Pastoral Leadership is often unseen and unappreciated publicly, yet hugely important. They sometimes feel threatened by the emphasis of the Pioneer and Strategist on "vision," and irritated by the Administrator's attention to detail, yet their contribution to a team is invaluable. Think for a moment of a Pastoral Leader who has made a difference in your life; you probably have considerable respect for that person.

Pastoral Leaders care little about vision or mission except when they can see how such things practically impact people in a positive way. There is nothing they love more than sitting face-to-face with others and sharing authentic life in Christ. They value one-on-one and small-group ministry. They are commonly characterized as warm, tender-hearted, sincere, kind, gentle and compassionate. Pastoral Leaders typically excel in perceiving the needs of others and listening with empathy—weeping when others weep and rejoicing when others rejoice (Rom. 12:15). For this reason Pastoral Leaders are often called to service in times of intense suffering, such as a serious illness or death, or during times of great celebration, such as a wedding.

In addition, Pastoral Leaders are commonly prayer warriors who consider their time alone with God as valuable as time spent with others. Intercessory prayer is a gift of the Holy Spirit granted to many Pastoral Leaders, and they should be strongly encouraged to exercise it for the sake of the mission and the mission team. The devil comes against anyone who seeks to be used in significant ways by Christ to advance His kingdom. Intercessory prayer is an essential element of a spiritually healthy and effective ministry team. In this respect, Pastoral Leaders may be the most significant and essential member of a ministry team.

Pastoral Leaders can and may lead missional groups or teams but are more likely to prefer interpersonal interaction and one-on-one influence. They are not at all task-focused; they value the individual above the task every time. For this reason they may better serve a team in a support role rather than a lead role. When Pastoral Leaders are placed in dominant leadership roles, the team may endure many meetings with much discussion, but little actual ministry is done. This is not because Pastoral Leaders are obstructionists! They want the work of ministry to go forward, but they are more concerned with the feelings and perspectives of all who are impacted by the ministry than with the mission itself.

The project synergy and momentum that Pioneering or Team Leaders believe to be essential to accomplishing a mission are often depleted by Pastoral Leaders over an extended period of time as they move the team forward slowly and cautiously. The ultimate goal of the Pastoral Leader is to minimize risk—the risk of failure and the risk of hurting others. However, sometimes they move a team so slowly that, like a bandage being removed slowly, they unintentionally extend the pain much longer. For this reason, while their motives may be pure, Pastoral Leaders may not practice the healthiest or most effective leadership methods.

The slower pace of the Pastoral Leader may create friction with other leader types such as Pioneers and Strategic Leaders, who value positive change and realize that synergy and momentum are often crucial allies in any serious project. But this relational stress can also be healthy; the Pastoral Leader provides a check-and-balance to the highly task-oriented leaders who might otherwise steamroll over people in their zeal to accomplish their missional objectives.

When a Pastoral Leader serves a team in a support role, caring for and nurturing others, the team is likely to be healthier spiritually and emotionally, and function more effectively. Under the Pastoral Leader's influence, team members begin to feel that their needs and concerns are being addressed, limiting the stresses that would otherwise result in relational conflict. A calming spirit and an ability to perceive and understand differing perspectives enables a Pastoral Leader to earn the respect and trust of each team member. Pastoral Leaders are by nature unifiers. They seek to be peacemakers and are unlikely to be the source of conflict, division and strife in a team or organization.

Because of the relational challenges of a team environment, Pastoral Leaders should have responsibility over the spiritual and emotional needs of the team. While they may have some administrative skills, Pastoral Leaders find managing data and tasks far more difficult than caring for people, and they should be protected from the stress of relational isolation in an office. The Pastoral Leader is fully equipped to pastor and encourage the team. The team needs a Pastoral Leader to counsel, encourage and lead the team emotionally, spiritually and relationally.

Pastoral Leaders need to realize that they cannot do it alone—they need the other members of their team, and the other team members need the Pastoral Leader. First Corinthians 12 affirms that the Body of Christ has many different members who all need one another and that God positions these members just as He has determined. God creates Pastoral Leaders and positions them strategically to nurture and support those who labor for the sake of Christ. The support of the Pastoral Leader will propel the kingdom of Christ forward to a world that desperately needs to know the power and love of the God who sent us His Spirit to comfort, nurture and guide God's people in their calling.

The Encouraging Leader

Highlights

- Sees the potential in people that others may overlook
- Supports people through close interpersonal relationships
- Is risk-avoidant and may be resistant to change
- Characterized typically by a quiet, reflective and gentle spirit
- May struggle with internal stress from empathizing with and carrying others' burdens

Report

Barnabas was a great encourager. When no one else believed that Saul (Paul) had truly changed from a persecutor to a follower of Jesus Christ, and had been called to be an Apostle, it was Barnabas who introduced Paul to the leaders of the Jerusalem church. Barnabas then became the primary supporter and encourager to Paul in his new ministry, traveling and suffering with him. In Acts 15:36 and following, we find that Paul had become disenchanted with a man by the name of Mark because Mark had abandoned them on an earlier mission trip. But Barnabas, an ever faithful encourager of the underdog, sought to include Mark on their upcoming missionary journey. Paul and Barnabas parted ways, and Barnabas, with Mark as his new partner, set off on his own missionary journey.

The nature of the Encouraging Leader is to see potential in people and nurture that potential until it becomes a reality. Where other leadership types may avoid certain people, deeming them unfit or ill-prepared to serve in ministry, the Encouraging Leader demonstrates the same grace that God extends to all who have failed—for we all have sinned and fall short of the glory of God. It is only by God's grace and nurture that any one of us is deemed by Him to be "fit" for ministry. The Encouraging Leader reflects this aspect of God's divine character.

Encouraging Leaders know when to give a quiet word to spur someone on, when to challenge, when to support, when to coach and when to give space. Occasionally they may irritate people by appearing less "involved" than other leadership styles; sometimes people want more than just encouragement. However, Encouraging Leaders excel at supporting individuals through close interpersonal relationships.

Relational depth is more valuable to an Encouraging Leader than relationships with many people. Encouraging Leaders are good listeners; they perceive, interpret and empathize with the thoughts and feelings of others. For this reason they make excellent personal consultants, counselors, hospital chaplains, visitation pastors and spiritual mentors.

Encouraging Leaders can make excellent small group leaders as well as recovery ministry leaders. They are not at all task-focused and should never be given the responsibility to lead a project to completion. Their focus is almost entirely on the people they serve. If asked to lead projects or task-oriented teams, Encouraging Leaders become anxious and stressed over details, and team meetings will likely be full of discussion with little ministry accomplished.

Encouraging Leaders want to know the thoughts, feelings and perspectives of each team member. They are not at all entrepreneurial and typically avoid risks, seeing them as potentially harmful to the people they value so deeply. They are peacemakers who seek to minimize or eliminate division, strife and stress in the lives of those they care about. They likely feel that change, if it must occur, should be enacted slowly and patiently.

The slower pace of the Encouraging Leader may create friction with other leader types such as Pioneers and Strategic Leaders, who value positive change and realize that synergy and momentum are often crucial allies in any serious project. But this relational stress can also be healthy; the Encouraging Leader provides a check-and-balance to the highly task-oriented leaders who might otherwise steamroll over people in their zeal to accomplish their missional objectives.

By nature, most Encouraging Leaders are quiet, reflective and gentle-spirited. Their reserved appearance conceals the depth of their emotional and thought life. While Pioneering or Strategic Leaders excel at analyzing the details and tasks of a project, Encouraging Leaders excel at analyzing people. Encouraging Leaders can quickly identify the strengths and weakness of an individual and focus on nurturing and supporting the individual's areas of personal struggle.

Ironically, while Encouraging Leaders are able to "size-up" people effectively, they themselves are not so easy to understand. They are complex individuals who may appear to others to place a low value on "getting the job done." If not properly understood and put to use within an organization, Encouraging Leaders may be seen as lazy or lacking in commitment. In fact, they are far from lazy and will work tirelessly in or, nurturing and supporting the emotional and spiritual needs of others.

Encouraging Leaders may perceive the tasks associated with ministry as a hindrance to "true" ministry to people and will avoid activities that limit their interactions with others. However, if they see that the only way to earn the trust and respect of someone is by "rolling up their shirt sleeves" and working alongside them, they will do so in hopes of establishing a relational bond.

Encouraging Leaders, more than any other leadership profile, may carry a lot of internal stress as they empathize with others' feelings and needs. The problems of others become, in a very real sense, their problems. They see themselves as carrying one another's burdens. This level of emotional and spiritual involvement is not something they can set aside at the end of the day. Such compartmentalization of life is an impossible dream to Encouraging Leaders, who often find themselves coming alongside needy people at all hours of the day or night.

This trait can cause Encouraging Leaders to worry about others, but this tendency can be redirected positively in intercessory prayer. Encouraging Leaders can be outstanding prayer warriors, which gives them much in common with Pastoral Leaders. A wise ministry will seek out Encouraging and Pastoral Leaders and charge them with the responsibility of leading and developing intercessory prayer teams.

Encouraging Leaders need to realize that they cannot do it alone— they need the other members of their team, and the other team members need the Encouraging Leader. First Corinthians 12 affirms that the Body of Christ has many different members who all need one another and that God positions these members just as He has determined. God creates Encouraging Leaders and positions them strategically to nurture and support the weak and wounded who have yet to complete their ministry for the sake of Christ. The support of the Encouraging Leader will propel the kingdom of Christ forward to a world that desperately needs to know the power and love of the God who sent us His Spirit to comfort and encourage God's people in their calling.

Spiritual Gift Reports

The following reports are also available within the *GraceGifts* assessment offered on-line from E-Church Essentials and AssessMe.org.

Administration

The gift of administration is the special ability to manage the affairs of the church and its respective ministries. People with this gift are highly effective at implementing and sustaining the mission and goals of the organization. Administrators tend to focus more on achieving goals and objectives than on nurturing people. Like Timothy in Philippians 2:19–22, Administrators can be self-sacrificing for the welfare of the organization. They tend to believe that the ministry and all its people will be served best when the organization functions optimally. Acts 6:1–7 tells us how the early church selected their first Administrators; their requirements included being "full of the Spirit and wisdom." Paul tells us in First Timothy 3:4–5, 12 that one thing the church should look for in potential leaders is the ability to "manage [their] family well." The passage continues: "If anyone does not know how to manage his own family, how can he take care of God's church?"

Application

The gift of administration can be shaped by the personality of the person who possesses the gift. As a result, people with the gift of Administration tend to fall into the following preferred roles (check all that may apply to your life and ministry):

____ *Content Administrators* are excellent detail people who prefer to focus on the business of the church or ministry project. They will naturally see all the details that must be addressed. This strength can be a wonderful asset to a ministry's stability and health when properly balanced so that the Content Administrator does not impede further ministry development because of "all the details." Content Administrators may have difficulty delegating details to others for fear that "balls will be dropped" or from an inner belief that "no one can do the job as well as I can"—and often their experience has proven to be correct.

____ *Organizational Administrators* excel at organizational systems and structures. They approach a complex project or organization and immediately begin to systematize it for maximum efficiency and ministry impact. They devise master strategic plans that make logical sense. However, it is important in implementing the strategic plan that Administrators not make others feel like pawns on a chessboard. Organizational Administrators are effective delegators of the details in the complex strategic plan.

____ *Human Resource Administrators* excel at people dynamics. They naturally think of both the individual's needs and also what that person adds to the overall team dynamic. While Human Resource Administrators value organizational structures and objectives, they also value people. People tend to trust and rely upon the Human Resource Administrator to seek their welfare as well as the welfare of the organization.

Creativity

It is God's nature to be creative, so it should come as no surprise that His spiritual gifts to His people would include this divine attribute. We ourselves are "God's workmanship, created in Christ Jesus to do good works, which God prepared in advance for us to do" (Eph. 2:10). By alluding to God as a creative master craftsman, Paul suggests in this passage that when God equips a person (with creativity or any other ability) it is His desire that the person use those abilities to accomplish specific ordained purposes. God created all things—and all things were created "for" Him (Col. 1:15–16).

Application

The gift of creativity, when used in the church, is shaped by the personality of the person who has the gift. As a result, people with the gift of creativity tend to fall into different roles. Select the areas in which you believe God could best use you in your situation:

____ *Communication Arts* includes oral and/or written communication skills. Within a ministry context, creative oral gifts can be utilized in various public speaking roles. Such roles might include preaching and teaching but may also include large-group leadership of children's or student ministries. With today's emerging technology, oral communication skills are also required for "on air" and "on-line" radio and television broadcast. Other, often overlooked roles may include comedy, master of ceremonies and ministry tour guides. Written communication arts include the development of song lyrics and poetry, script writing, newsletters and content authoring for websites and reading materials. With the emergence of e-learning within the church, people with creative communication gifts will now be in even greater demand.

____ *Craftsmanship Arts* are typically found in "Artisan" personalities (see the ePersonality assessment). Craftsmen like to work with their hands, creating something from nothing. Woodcraft, metalcraft, sculpture, painting, sewing and software programming are all hands-on arts that require expertise and skill.

____ *Graphic Arts* (computer based) have become a necessity for the contemporary and postmodern ministry. Graphic artists work on printed materials, multi-media presentations, video, website design, etc. If a picture is worth a thousand words, it is no wonder that ministries are seeking to communicate more effectively through the graphic arts.

____ *Musical Arts* are in great demand within church ministries. Gifted worship leaders are among the most sought-after ministry staff roles in North America. The Bible makes many references to the "Chief Musician" and the role of thousands of musicians (called gatekeepers) in Old Testament temple worship. The first thing that worshippers approaching the temple in Jerusalem encountered was a giant musical praise team outside the temple gates, charged with the responsibility of playing and singing songs of praise and thanksgiving from morning until evening of each day! The musical arts are intended by God to help people to praise and worship Him (See 1 Chron. 9:33, 23:5–6; 2 Chron. 29:25–30, 31:2; Ps. 100:4; Eph. 5:18–19).

____ *Performing Arts* are creative expressions that bring to life the issues and emotions of our everyday reality. The use of drama and/or dance within a worship service can help attendees connect to the topic or theme being addressed within the service program. Performing Artists are uniquely able to help us connect with the characters of the dance or drama. They are most effective when they hold a mirror up to our lives, enabling us to remove the mask from our own lives and see who we really are and who God wants us to be.

____ *Relational Arts* can be easily overlooked, yet they address one of the toughest aspects of ministry—the art of relationship-building. Relational Artists are impeccable hosts. They know how to throw a party, but more importantly, they know how to make everyone at that party feel welcome and wanted. Relational Artists thrive at networking people with people. People-skills, manners, appropriateness and tact are defining traits of the Relational Artist.

____ *Technical Arts* are crucial to the contemporary and postmodern ministry. Sound, lighting, multimedia, computer technology, software, networking and Internet-based ministry are all areas that require this non-traditional creative artist. With the advent of the Internet and e-church ministry, the Technical Artist will find more and more opportunities to unleash his or her skill and creativity.

_____ *Visual Arts* involve an "eye" for presentation. The Visual Artist may be an interior decorator, floral arranger, stage and set designer, lighting director, etc. They may excel at drawing, painting or photography. Our present culture acquires information through the eyes much more effectively than through the ears. The Visual Artist is uniquely gifted to help pastoral teachers to communicate more effectively by integrating the visual arts into their messages and programs.

Spiritual Discernment

Spiritual Discernment is a special ability to sense the presence of godly and demonic spiritual forces. This is an important gift for the church because often the work of Satan can appear on the surface to be very positive. Without discernment, Satan could easily lead many people away from Christ. The Apostle Paul specifically lists "discerning of spirits" among the spiritual gifts (1 Cor. 12:10). First John 4:1–6 instructs the church to "test the spirits." Acts 16:16–19 relates how the Apostle Paul used the gift of "discerning of spirits" when he encountered a slave girl who was possessed by an evil spirit masquerading as a spirit of light.

Application

The gift of Spiritual Discernment does not typically fit into "office" positions. However, within the context of church ministry, this gift is a valuable asset to the following ministry functions. Select the areas in which you believe God could best use you in your situation:

_____ *Restoration and Recovery Ministry.* Restoration and recovery ministries often address serious spiritual strongholds and bondage issues that have dominated a person's life for many years. The ability to discern between habitual or chemical dependency problems and spiritual problems is an important distinction.

___ *Instructional Accountability Ministry.* Is what is taught in the church truly of the Lord and confirmed by Scripture? Spiritual Discernment is often needed to ensure the health and welfare of the Body. In the Matthew 4 narrative, it is clear that Satan knows and quotes the Bible. Not every "good" word is a "godly" word. The prophet Jeremiah was commissioned by God to deliver a tough message of discipline to God's people while other "prophets" were expounding a future of peace and prosperity (Jer. 14:13–14). We are told that "in later times some will abandon the faith and follow deceiving spirits and things taught by demons. Such teachings come through hypocritical liars, whose consciences have been seared as with a hot iron" (1 Tim. 4:1–2). Paul also instructs Timothy that "the time will come when men will not put up with sound doctrine. Instead, to suit their own desires, they will gather around them a great number of teachers to say what their itching ears want to hear. They will turn their ears away from the truth and turn aside to myths" (2 Tim. 4:3–4). Those who seek to properly use the gift of Spiritual Discernment in a ministry of instructional accountability must be sure they know their Bible well and test all judgments by the Word of God.

___ *Front Line Evangelism Ministry.* In spiritual warfare, as in any warfare, the real battles take place at the front lines. The ministry of evangelism seeks to rescue people who knowingly or unknowingly serve the Evil One and help them become followers of Jesus Christ. The Apostle Paul tells us that "the weapons we fight with are not the weapons of the world. On the contrary, they have divine power to demolish strongholds. We demolish arguments and every pretension that sets itself up against the knowledge of God" (2 Corinthians 10:4–5).

It may not always be clear if particular people are Christians or not. They may go to church, perhaps all their life. They may say the right words or act the right way. But this does not make a person right with God. Only true faith in the work of Jesus Christ, evidenced by the sanctifying and gifting work of the Holy Spirit, enables a person to be "in Christ." Spiritual Discernment can clarify a person's spiritual state and help identify their roadblocks to faith. The Apostle Peter demonstrated Spiritual Discernment in Acts 5:3–5 in dealing with the lies and false faith exhibited by Ananias and Sapphira. In Acts 8:18–23 Peter again demonstrates Spiritual Discernment regarding the spiritual health of Simon the Sorcerer—that he was "full of bitterness and captive to sin."

_____ *Counseling Ministry.* Today, counseling ministries tend to take a holistic approach toward those they serve, ministering to the mind, emotions and spirit. It is the "spirit" aspect of counseling where Spiritual Discernment can be of great value. The spiritual state of a person has a great impact on their emotional and mental well-being. Having the gift of Spiritual Discernment does not *by itself* qualify one to be a counselor of others; additional gifts and professional training are needed. However, the gift of Spiritual Discernment can help a counselor identify a person's spiritual condition.

Disciple-Maker

A person possessing the gift of Disciple-Maker is generally concerned with the healthy spiritual development of people in their circle of influence. A Disciple-Maker often displays the ministry traits of Pastor and Teacher, and prefers to minister to small groups or within a one-on-one mentoring relationship. The Disciple-Maker is skilled at developing deep interpersonal relationships, values Biblical knowledge and likes to help others identify and achieve spiritual development goals.

Application

Depending upon the personality traits of the Disciple-Maker, he or she will usually prefer to use their gift in one of the following three ways:

_____*Pastoral Shepherding.* Pastoral Shepherding has more to do with caring for and nurturing small groups of Christ-followers than it does with "running a church." Shepherds passionately care for the welfare of the group as well as the individuals that comprise the group. In Acts 20:27–32 Paul gives his instructions to the Ephesian pastoral leaders: "Guard yourselves and all the flock of which the Holy Spirit has made you overseers. Be shepherds of the church of God, which he bought with his own blood."

___*Biblical Instructor.* Biblical instructors care about people but prefer to focus on communicating Biblical concepts and truths *to* people. Biblical Instructors make excellent Bible study leaders, Sunday school teachers and small group leaders (when the need of the small group is for instruction rather than pastoral care). In Acts 8:26–40, Philip utilizes his gift of Disciple-Maker in an instructor capacity when he conducts a Bible study with the Ethiopian leader.

___*Personal Mentorship.* Mentors invest their lives in others. They prefer intense one-on-one relationships. They feel a personal responsibility for the spiritual welfare of their disciples. The account of Priscilla, Aquila and Apollos in Acts 18:24–28 is an excellent example of personal mentorship. Pricilla and Aquila invited Apollos to live with them while they mentored and instructed him. This intense mentorship was just what Apollos needed to be Biblically and spiritually prepared to support the ministry of the Apostle Paul.

Encouragement

A person with the gift of Encouragement has a unique ability to help others gain a positive emotional and spiritual perspective on their circumstances. Encouragers are people who find the positive in any situation. For them, "the glass is always half full." Encouragers are at their best when they can motivate the assembly of Christ-followers to persevere in the struggle against sin and to strive for the accomplishment of God's mission for the church. The word encouragement means "to instill courage into another person."

Romans 12:8 and Hebrews 10:24–25 instruct all Christ-followers to "encourage one another." This gift of encouragement is clearly exemplified in the life of a man named Joseph, first mentioned in Acts 4:36–37. Joseph sold all that he had and laid the money at the feet of the Apostles. At that point, Joseph's name was changed to *Barnabas*— "Son of Encouragement." In Acts 9:26–27 we learn that when all the disciples were afraid of Paul (Saul) and questioned whether his conversion was real, it was Barnabas that risked his own life to visit Paul and to introduce him to the body of believers. In Acts 13 the Holy

Spirit instructed the church at Antioch to set apart Paul and Barnabas for a special missionary work—and so Barnabas became Paul's ministry partner.

Application

Following Barnabas's encouragement roles, we can identify three major ways in which the gift of Encouragement may express itself within the church (your personality style and calling from the Holy Spirit may enable you to focus the use of your gift):

___*Sacrificing Self for Welfare of Others.* Barnabas sold all he had for the welfare of others within the church. Encouragement is best received by others when the Encourager will not receive any personal benefit from the encouragement offered. There are many hurt and damaged people in this sinful world. They have been "used and abused." Their level of trust in others is minimal. Sacrificial encouragement can help restore and heal.

___*Supporting Risky Ministry Ventures.* New ministry ventures are risky. Often those who attempt to begin a new church, ministry or mission have many critics who add their voices to the chorus of doubt and fear that may already linger in the minds of these risk-takers. They need to be reminded that God is in control and that nothing that is of God will ever fail. There is no greater encouragement to the ministry trailblazer than when an Encourager gets personally involved and "takes the risk" with everyone else. Encouragers possesses significant confidence in the nature and purposes of God. Like Barnabas, Encouragers can often take the risks that others are afraid to take.

___*Serving Ministry Leadership.* Leadership is lonely and emotionally draining. Everyone wants to receive from ministry leaders, but very few seek to minister to them. Encouragers are essential to the success of any ministry leader.

Evangelism

All Christ-followers are responsible to evangelize, but people with the gift of Evangelism display exceptional boldness and skill at sharing their faith. They often share their faith as a natural part of any conversation and may even find it common to share their faith with complete strangers. Evangelists can list the specific names of people whom they have personally led to faith in Christ.

Ephesians 4:11–13 lists Evangelist not only as a spiritual gift but also as an important office in the church which God has ordained "to prepare God's people for works of service, so that the body of Christ may be built up until we all reach unity in the faith and in the knowledge of the Son of God and become mature, attaining to the whole measure of the fullness of Christ." The Evangelist shares this God-ordained commission with Apostles, Prophets, Pastors and Teachers, but without the work of the Evangelist, those in other ministry offices could not fulfill their calling. Unless a person first comes to know Jesus Christ as their Lord and Savior, it is pointless to consider how they will "become mature" in Christ.

Application

In today's ministries Evangelism is generally utilized in two ways: 1) Programmed Evangelism and 2) Personal Evangelism. Based upon your distinct personality, select all that apply:

____*Programmed Evangelism.* Programmed evangelism centers around "seeker events" such as seeker services, evangelism crusades or evangelistic Bible studies. Programmed evangelism utilizes the gifts and abilities of many people to accomplish the work of communicating the gospel. The Evangelist who prefers programmed evangelism will likely be highly creative or, in contrast, have strong administrative skills. They may also be "big picture" people who seek many conversions to Christ and do not have the patience for one-on-one evangelism as their primary ministry. In Acts 17:16–34 the Apostle Paul used programmed evangelism when he entered the meeting of the Areopagus in which the Epicurean and Stoic philosophers debated new ideas every day. Paul introduced a new idea for discussion: the "unknown God" who raises the dead to life. The result was that a few influential philosophers believed in Jesus Christ.

___*Personal Evangelism.* If God has given you a highly relational personality, you will likely prefer personal evangelism. These Evangelists can be found wherever people gather. They seek to build authentic relationships and through those relationships share the gospel one-on-one. They are thrilled to be able to personally pray with an individual to receive Christ. They grow to care deeply for the spiritual welfare of the people God has brought into their life and may spend considerable time praying for the salvation of those that do not know the Lord. The Personal Evangelist will resonate with the passion of the Apostle Paul:

> "All this is from God, who reconciled us to himself through Christ and gave us the ministry of reconciliation: that God was reconciling the world to himself in Christ, not counting men's sins against them. And he has committed to us the message of reconciliation. We are therefore Christ's ambassadors, as though God were making his appeal through us. We implore you on Christ's behalf: Be reconciled to God" (2 Corinthians 5:18–20).

Exhortation

The gift of Exhortation is the special ability to counsel or challenge others toward a healthy relationship with Jesus Christ. Often the gift is utilized to motivate the church in general or a Christ-follower in particular to make God-honoring choices. If those gifted with Exhortation do not learn sensitivity and tact, they may not immediately be appreciated. The gift of Exhortation is somewhat similar to the role of the Old Testament prophets in challenging God's people to remain faithful. While the prophets were not immediately valued, and often persecuted, their service was indispensable to the spiritual health and vitality of the Biblical faith community.

People with the gift of Exhortation will not avoid conflict. It is not that they love conflict—in fact, they may hate it—but they feel a deep responsibility before God to challenge and encourage those that may be taking a path that does not honor the Lord, to correct their misguided choices. In Acts 14:22 the Apostle Paul strove to "strengthen the disciples and to encourage them to remain true to the faith." In Acts 11:23 Barnabas encouraged the people of Antioch to remain true to the Lord with all their hearts. And Paul describes his ministry among the Thessalonians as "encouraging, comforting and urging you to live lives worthy of God, who calls you into his kingdom and glory" (1 Thess. 2:12).

The gift of Exhortation is always expressed in a personal appeal— even when focused on a group. The group is made up of individuals who are responsible for their own decisions and actions before God. This is why people often react defensively when first hearing a word of exhortation. When this gift is utilized appropriately, it will either be received by humble and contrite hearts, or with hostility and transference. Those who exercise the gift of Exhortation may be accused of being judgmental, critical or harsh, so they should be sure that "how" they communicate does not get in the way of "what" they communicate on God's behalf. However even a word of exhortation delivered carefully and lovingly may be initially rejected—along with the one who communicated the message. People with the gift of Exhortation quickly learn that they need to give the Holy Spirit an opportunity to do His work of conviction and sanctification.

Exorcism

The gift of Exorcism is the special ability to confront demonic forces in the lives of spiritually oppressed people and to help such people find spiritual freedom in Christ Jesus. People with the gift of Exorcism may also display the gifts of Spirit Discernment and Intercessory Prayer. An Exorcist conducts spiritual warfare prayer and helps oppressed people understand their freedom, authority and identity in Christ Jesus. Through direct confrontation of demonic spirits, they help others gain freedom through the name and authority of Jesus Christ. There are many passages that describe the gift of Exorcism in practice. Luke 10:16–24, Acts 16:18 and Luke 11:14–28 are but a few.

Faith

Every Christ-follower has established a relationship with God through faith in the work and person of Jesus Christ. However, the gift of Faith enables a person to trust God even more so for remarkable provision, especially in circumstances that appear to offer no viable solution. The person gifted with Faith often displays unusual confidence in the will and purposes of God and communicates to others peace and assurance. People gifted with Faith may become frustrated with others, even church leaders, for moving too slowly or for supporting a limited vision or easily obtained goals. People gifted with Faith know that God wants to do more through us than we could think or imagine (Eph. 3:20).

Application

First Corinthians 12:9 specifically identifies Faith within its list of gifts granted by the Holy Spirit. Hebrews 11 portrays a lineage of people who possessed great faith in God. James 2:22–24 makes it clear that true faith will be evidenced in the actions of those who claim to have faith. In the church, Faith can find expression in many ways. However, based on your personality type, you may be more inclined to utilize this gift of Faith in one of the following ways:

___*Faith for Physical, Emotional or Spiritual Restoration.* When the gift of faith is used in this manner, the person possessing the gift of faith may also possess the gift of Healing, Spiritual Discernment or Intercessory Prayer.

___*Faith for Financial or Material Provision.* When the gift of Faith is used this way, the gifted person may also have the gift of giving, stewardship or encouragement. Those with the gift of Faith expressed in financial or material provision will likely exercise this gift in personal giving well above their tithe. In addition, when they see a person or family in need, they are likely to extend themselves to meet that need.

___*Faith for Risky Ministry Opportunities.* People with the gift of Faith are often frustrated when they see people and ministries taking small, manageable risks for Christ's kingdom. They know that God can do more than we think or imagine. People with the gift of Faith can dream big because they are enabled by the Holy Spirit to trust big.

For this reason, this type of gifted person will gravitate to roles and leaders who desire to accomplish great things for the Kingdom.

Giving

The gift of Giving is a special enabling from God to give sacrificially of finances, time and talents toward the work of God. People with this gift may also display the gift of Faith or Stewardship. The gift of Giving is often exercised in free-will offerings well in excess of the Biblical tithe. It is not uncommon for people with this gift to testify that the more they give to God, the more God blesses them so that they are able to give again.

The Apostle Paul lists the gift of Giving among other gifts in Romans 12:8. In Second Corinthians 8:1–7, Paul commends the Macedonian church to all the other churches because of the special grace God had given them to give to others out of their poverty.

Application

The gift of Giving is generally expressed in three areas of life: Finances, Time and Talents. Please select the categories that you most identify with.

___*Giving of Resources.* Whether God has blessed you financially, or like the Macedonians, you are called to give from out of your poverty—either way, you believe God has called you to give of your financial resources for the work of ministry.

___*Giving of Time.* Time is a valuable resource and gift from God. It is often far easier to write a check to meet a need than it is to invest personal time. You believe God has gifted you to invest your time to support others.

___*Giving of Abilities.* God has given all of us many skills and talents, which differ from spiritual gifts in that we have developed them since childhood. You believe God has called you to give of your talents for His glory.

Healing

The gift of healing is the ability given by God to pray over the sick and have them made well. The healing may be instantaneous or take place over time, but it is accomplished in a way that gives the credit to God, not man. A person with the gift of healing may also have the gifts of Faith and/or Evangelism.

In First Corinthians 12:9, 28, the Apostle Paul lists Healing as one of many gifts granted by the Holy Spirit. In James 5:13–20, the Church is instructed to pray over the sick and the prayer of faith will make them well. In Acts 9:32–35 we find one of many examples of instantaneous healing accomplished by the Holy Spirit through the Apostle Peter. The earthly ministry of Jesus was marked by His ability to heal, and He said, "I tell you the truth, anyone who has faith in me will do what I have been doing. He will do even greater things than these, because I am going to the Father. And I will do whatever you ask in my name, so that the Son may bring glory to the Father. You may ask me for anything in my name, and I will do it" (John 14:12–14).

Helps/Service

The gift of Helps is sometimes also called the gift of Service or Mercy. The mark of this spiritual gift is a passion to humbly serve and support others in the assembly of believers. The person with the gift of Service displays a natural servant's heart and seeks the welfare of others, even to the point of self-sacrifice. It is not uncommon for people with the gift of Helps to feel that they don't have any gifts at all, but this is far from true. When this gift is applied in the body of Christ, the helper is acting much like Jesus, who said of His own ministry, "I did not come to be served, but to serve" (Matt. 20:28). Paul speaks honorably about Phoebe who had the gift of Helps: "I commend to you our sister Phoebe, a servant of the church in Cenchrea. I ask you to receive her in the Lord in a way worthy of the saints and give her any help she may need from you, for she has been a great help to many people, including me" (Rom. 16:1–2). In First Corinthians 12:27–31, Paul also lists "helping others" among the "greater gifts." First Peter 4:11 tells us, "If any one serves, he should do it in the strength that God provides."

Application

Depending upon your personality type, you may prefer one of two ways to apply your gift of Helps (select the one that applies to you):

___*I prefer to help individuals.* You may feel a particular passion to use your gift of Helps within the lives of individuals. You prefer one-on-one interaction. You like to see tangible results from the direct impact God is making through you in the lives of others.

___*I prefer to help ministry teams.* You may feel that you best fit within a positive team environment. You prefer not to be alone and value the support and camaraderie that can only be experienced in partnership with others for the sake of the Kingdom. In addition, you may also view yourself as a "resource" person who likes to make sure everyone on the ministry team has what they need to be successful.

Intercessory Prayer

While God desires all Christ-followers to communicate with Him through regular prayer, those with the gift of Intercessory Prayer are specially endowed by the Holy Spirit as "Prayer Warriors" for the sake of other people and ministries. They stand on the front lines of spiritual warfare. Because this gift is usually exercised in private, it is often overlooked in the church, but without "Prayer Warriors" many visible ministry efforts would probably not be successful.

Biblical examples and instruction regarding Intercessory Prayer include Epaphras, whom Paul said "is always wrestling in prayer for you, that you may stand firm in all the will of God, mature and fully assured" (Col. 4:12–13). Paul describes his own exercise of the gift as well: "For this reason, since the day we heard about you, we have not stopped praying for you and asking God to fill you with the knowledge of his will through all spiritual wisdom and understanding" (Col. 1:9). In First Timothy 2:1 Paul states: "I urge, then, first of all, that requests, prayers, intercession and thanksgiving be made for everyone."

Interpretation of Tongues

The Bible makes it clear that the use of Tongues within a corporate gathering of Christ-followers should be accompanied by a person with the gift of Interpretation of Tongues so that the whole body may benefit (1 Cor. 14:5, 26–28). In First Corinthians 12:10, the Apostle Paul lists Interpretation of Tongues among the many available gifts. In verse 30 of this same passage, Paul makes it clear that this gift is not available to everyone. When a person with the gift of Tongues partners with a person with the gift of Interpretation of Tongues to minister in a gathering, their joint ministries serve much the same function as the gift of Prophecy.

Leadership

The gift of Leadership is the God-given ability to lead people to accomplish God's vision and goals. The Biblical image used when describing leadership is "shepherd." A Shepherd does not force his will upon the sheep; rather he tends and cares for them. The sheep instinctively follow a good shepherd. Jesus describes himself as the "Good Shepherd," and calls church leaders His "Under Shepherds." The "Under Shepherds" must faithfully follow the example of the "Good Shepherd" and lay their lives down for the welfare of the sheep (John 10:14–18). The person gifted by God with Leadership will display the same servant leadership principles evidenced by Jesus and the Apostles.

Leaders within the church are held to a higher standard before God: "Remember your leaders, who spoke the word of God to you. Consider the outcome of their way of life and imitate their faith. . . . Obey your leaders and submit to their authority. They keep watch over you as men who must give an account" (Heb. 13:7–17). In First Timothy 5:20 the Apostle Paul stresses that "(Leaders) who sin are to be rebuked publicly, so that others may take warning."

Application

Depending upon your personality type, you likely prefer to utilize your leadership gifts in one of the following Leadership Style Categories. (select all that may apply to you):

___*Pioneering Leadership.* Pioneering leaders are willing to push themselves and take appropriate risks, striving to discover and reach long-term goals, "forgetting what is behind, and straining for what lies ahead" (Phil. 3:13). Pioneering leaders are passionate and wholly committed to a vision. Paul is a great example of a leader who was focused on pushing out the boundaries of the church despite the personal risk. Pioneering leaders are at their strongest in the early stages of a vision or project, excited by seeking out where God is calling. As time passes they may lose interest in implementing a vision and be eager to go on to the next challenge.

___*Strategic Leadership.* Leaders who can break down visions and large aims into manageable chunks are vital for the church. Strategic leaders have the insight and focus to work out ways of achieving the vision (the "how") and are able to persuade the rest of the church to accept this plan. When Nehemiah led the Jews in rebuilding the walls of Jerusalem, he demonstrated great strategic leadership in delegating the work. The result was that the walls were rebuilt in 52 days. Strategic leaders can bring common sense to difficult tasks. They are able to help people see how the seemingly impossible can be achieved. However, like Pioneers, they can be less engaged with the implementation of a task, preferring to leave this to others.

___*Management/Administration.* All churches require good stewards and managers, people with gifts of administration (Acts 6). Any vision or change requires people who can plan, solve problems, delegate and organize. Without this gift the best plans may not get implemented! The apostles delegated the practical tasks of sharing food and taking care of the widows to those gifted with the necessary skills, including Stephen and Philip. Managers are often under-appreciated, having a leadership style which is less "up-front" than some of the other styles. However, much of the work simply would not get done without them. They are able to organize and follow through on all the necessary tasks and activities to ensure that projects are completed on time. They may struggle to relate to the visionary pioneers; dreaming of achieving the impossible is not their home ground!

___*Team Leadership.* Team Leaders influence groups whether they have a formal leadership role in the group or not. For the church as "the body" (1 Cor. 12), working together is clearly important. The key strengths of team leaders are a desire to work with others and an ability to trust them. Team Leaders need great humility and servanthood—their sole aim is that the team achieves its goals. What they as individuals achieve is secondary. The greatest contribution Silas made to the church was probably training and equipping Paul, who went on to achieve greater things. Team leaders are invaluable. If the church is truly to function as a body, team leaders are needed to ensure harmony and effectiveness in the way the team works.

___*Pastoral Leadership.* Many church leaders feel they ought to be pastoral leaders, though they may not have this as their primary style. Pastoral leaders are real "people-people," who have an important role in supporting the pioneers, strategists, team leaders and the rest of the church, particularly when times are hard. Vision and moving into vision seem less important to pastoral leaders. Peter was a pastoral leader, a complete contrast to Paul's energetic church planting and exhortation. Pastoral leadership is often unseen, and often unappreciated publicly, yet hugely important. Those who are pastoral leaders can sometimes feel threatened by the pioneers and strategists. At times they are irritated by the attention to detail shown by the managers. Yet their contribution to a team is invaluable. Take a moment to think of a pastoral leader, and you will probably find that they command huge respect and support.

___*Encouraging Leadership.* Paul was a great encourager; his letters to the early churches contained exhortation and encouragement as well as teaching. Encouraging leaders are able to motivate whole churches, teams and individuals. They have great discernment into people's gifts, feelings and motivations, and are able to release them to fulfill their ministries. (Who *doesn't* need encouragement?) Encouraging leaders have a knack of knowing when to give a quiet word to spur someone on, when to challenge, when to support, when to coach and when to give space. Occasionally they may irritate people by appearing less "involved" than other leadership styles—sometimes people want more than just encouragement.

Musical Expression/Worship

The gift of Worship enables a person to lead others, by way of example, to seek the heart of God. All Christ-followers are called by God to worship Him. Those with the gift of Worship and Musical Expression, however, seem to know how to guide the emotions and spirits of others so that they forget their surroundings and circumstances, and focus on the greatness of God.

Old Testament temple worship had a category of Levites called doorkeepers. Doorkeepers were responsible for the various entrances of the temple. Among the doorkeepers were a large number of Levites who were gifted in Worship and Musical Expression. Their job was to serve outside the main entrance to the temple as a giant worship team, playing and singing songs of praise and thanksgiving. And so we find Psalm 100:4 exclaiming: "Enter his gates with thanksgiving and his courts with praise; give thanks to him and praise his name." Over 4,000 worship team members served in rotation, providing songs of praise and thanksgiving from sunrise to sunset. This large worship team was led by a person with the title of "Chief Musician." We find that many of the psalms were written by or for the Chief Musician (See 1 Chron. 25:1, 6–8; 2 Chron. 5:12–14, 2 Chron. 29:25–30).

Jesus proclaimed that "a time is coming and has now come when true worshipers will worship the Father in spirit and truth, for they are the kind of worshipers the Father seeks" (John 4:23–24). Paul further instructs the church, "Let the word of Christ dwell in you richly as you teach and admonish one another with all wisdom, and as you sing psalms, hymns and spiritual songs with gratitude in your hearts to God" (Col. 3:16).

Application

If you feel led by God to serve Him and others in Worship and Musical Expression, please check the appropriate areas in which you might serve:

___ Worship Leader   ___ Lead Vocalist, Baritone

___ Lead Vocalist, Tenor   ___ Lead Vocalist, Alto

___ Lead Vocalist, Soprano   ___ Support Vocalist, Bass

___ Support Vocalist, Baritone   ___ Support Vocalist, Tenor

___ Support Vocalist, Alto   ___ Support Vocalist, Soprano

___ Musician, Keyboards   ___ Musician, Acoustic Guitar

___ Musician, Electric Guitar   ___ Musician, Bass Guitar

___ Musician, Percussion   ___ Musician, Strings

___ Musician, Brass   ___ Musician, Woodwinds

___ Other _____

New Ministry Developer

This is an entrepreneurial gift that enables people to develop new ministries, churches or missions. New ministry developers are risk-takers for the kingdom of God. They are always seeking new territories in which to start outreach ministries and are on the forefront of new ministry development within the established local church. Those with this gift are dissatisfied with the status quo in church ministry. They are always seeking new and better ways to accomplish the work of the gospel.

The Apostle Paul was definitely called by God to be a new ministry developer. He describes his role in this way: "By the grace God has given me, I laid a foundation as an expert builder, and someone else is building on it" (1 Cor. 3:10). Paul also said, "It has always been my ambition to preach the gospel where Christ was not known, so that I would not be building on someone else's foundation" (Rom. 15:20).

Application

Depending on your personality style, you may prefer one of the following applications of your gift of New Ministry Developer (select all that may apply to you):

___ *Church Planter.* A Church Planter seeks to develop new churches in regions where there are few or none. Church Planters are typically sensitive to regional demographics, growth trends and church-per-capita statistics. They are passionate about evangelism and reaching the unreached by extending ministry into new territories.

___ *Cross-Cultural Missionary.* Cross-cultural missions may not always be overseas ministry, though this is the classic ministry role. In today's cultural melting pot, it may mean extending an outreach ministry to a different community across town. Cross-cultural missionaries are sensitive to cultural distinctives as well as the value of cultural diversity. They are typically passionate about living out the ministry ideal of "the unity of the body of Christ." Cross-cultural missionaries are also typically passionate about the work of evangelism.

___ *New e-Church Ministries.* E-church ministry (ministry via the internet) is still a new and developing ministry medium. Attempting to define e-church ministry is difficult at best. However, proponents of e-church ministry tend to value freedom of expression and safe spiritual exploration. They tend to be passionate about the work of evangelism as well as mentoring people in their spiritual formation. They also tend to value cultural diversity and be technically astute.

___ *New Campus Ministries.* There is always room for new campus-based ministries within an established church. People called and equipped by God to develop new campus-based ministries tend to be sensitive to groups of people who are "slipping through the cracks," as well as those to whom the ministry is not yet properly positioned to minister. New campus ministry developers typically desire to take their local church to the "next level" in its ministry development. They are dissatisfied with the status quo.

___ *New Community Impact Ministries.* New community impact ministry developers are typically passionate about social justice and social impact within their community in the name of Christ. City missions, food pantries and shelters are classic examples of community impact ministries. Contemporary examples include computer training centers, vocational training, "random acts of kindness," after-school care centers, etc.

Pastor

The gift of Pastor is also an office of authority within the church. A Pastor is gifted by God to develop long-term relationships with a group of Christ-followers and assumes responsibility for their spiritual development and personal nurture. A Pastor guides, instructs, encourages, exhorts and at times disciplines members of the assembly of Christ-followers. Ephesians 4:11–12 makes it clear that the Pastor is particularly called of God to equip lay people to utilize their spiritual gifts in personal ministry. When the gift of Pastor is publicly recognized, and a person with this gift is elevated to the office of pastor, the "pastor" is also considered by the Bible to be an "Overseer" or "Elder" of the local congregation. First Peter 5:1–11 and First Timothy 3:1–7 provide instructions regarding the selection, qualifications and operations of an Elder/Overseer.

Application

A person with the gift of Pastor will express that gift differently based upon their God-given personality. You may find that you prefer one or more of the following expressions of the pastoral gift (select all that may apply to your personal life and ministry):

____ *Nurturing Pastor.* Pastoral care often involves nurturing and caring for weak members of the body, typically as a one-on-one ministry. Visiting the sick and shut-ins, caring for a small group or comforting those who suffer are all classic functions of a Nurturing Pastor.

____ *Teaching Pastor.* Teaching Pastors prefer to study the Word of God and expound it for others within the Body. Paul instructed Timothy to "Preach the Word; be prepared in season and out of season; correct, rebuke and encourage—with great patience and careful instruction. For the time will come when men will not put up with sound doctrine" (2 Tim. 4:2–3). He also gave this counsel to Pastoral Teachers: "Do not go beyond what is written" (1 Cor. 4:6). And James issued this warning: "Not many of you should presume to be teachers, my brothers, because you know that we who teach will be judged more strictly" (James 3:1).

____ *Administrative Pastor.* Most personality types that God generally calls into pastoral roles are people-people and so are typically weak strategic planners and system administrators. However, there exists a category of people to whom God does grant the gift of "Pastor," and while they do care for people, they are called to focus their service upon the systems and structures of the ministry. They possess strong administrative and planning abilities and so are able to help other pastoral types be less reactive in their ministry. The Administrative Pastor's ability to proactively plan and create ministry systems enables other pastoral ministry types to be more effective. These same qualities are essential in establishing a broad-based lay ministry within the church. Administrative Pastors seek to empower others and delegate responsibility.

____ *Evangelistic Pastor.* An Evangelistic Pastor generally has the gift of Evangelism as well as Pastor. The Evangelism Pastor is passionate about ministry to spiritual seekers. Typically, the "Pastoral" aspect of their gifts and personality cause them to prefer relational rather than programmed approaches to the work of Evangelism.

____ *Discipleship Pastor.* The Discipleship Pastor is concerned about spiritual formation in the lives of people. They value working with people at every stage of spiritual development from seeker to leader.

Prophecy

The gift of Prophecy is the unique ability to receive messages from God and communicate those messages to the assembly of Christ-followers. The ability to communicate divine messages may take the form of pastoral preaching, Word of Knowledge, Tongues with Interpretation of Tongues or foretelling future events. The words of a Prophet will always be supported by the principles and teachings of Scripture.

Application

Depending on your personality type and unique mix of gifts, you may prefer to utilize your gift of Prophecy in the following ways (check all areas that may apply):

___ *Pastoral Preaching.* Teaching Pastors prefer to study and expound the Word of God for others within the Body. Paul instructed Timothy to "Preach the Word; be prepared in season and out of season; correct, rebuke and encourage—with great patience and careful instruction. For the time will come when men will not put up with sound doctrine" (2 Timothy 4:2–3). He also gave this counsel to Pastoral Teachers: "Do not go beyond what is written" (1 Corinthians 4:6). And James issued this warning: "Not many of you should presume to be teachers, my brothers, because you know that we who teach will be judged more strictly" (James 3:1).

___ *Word of Knowledge.* The gift of Knowledge is a special insight given by God regarding His will applied to a particular circumstance.

___ *Tongues with Interpretation of Tongues.* The gift of Tongues, used in the assembly of believers, enables a Christ-follower to receive divine messages from God for the benefit of the assembly. Practice of Tongues in the assembly is limited in use by Scripture to those occasions when a person gifted with the Interpretation of Tongues is available to interpret the message.

___ *Foretelling Future Events.* Acts 21:10–11 is an excellent example of Prophecy as foretelling events. In this passage a prophet named Agabus took Paul's belt, tied his own hands and feet with it and said, "The Holy Spirit says, 'In this way the Jews of Jerusalem will bind the owner of this belt and will hand him over to the Gentiles.'"

Stewardship

The gift of Stewardship is the God-enabled ability to manage financial, human and time resources effectively in a manner that honors the Lord. Those with the gift of Stewardship may also display the gift of administration and/or the gift of Giving. Jesus defined good stewardship in Luke 12:42–44: "The Lord answered, 'Who then is the faithful and wise manager, whom the master puts in charge of his servants to give them food allowance at the proper time? It will be good for that servant whom the master finds doing so when he returns. I tell you the truth he will put him in charge of all his possessions.'" Similarly, the Parable of the Talents (Matt. 25:14–30) makes it clear that the wise steward will invest and multiply whatever God has given him.

Application

Based upon your personality style and mix of gifts, you may prefer to use your gift of Stewardship in the following ways (select all that apply to your life and ministry):

____ *Manager of Ministry Finances.* I believe God has used my training, experience and abilities to prepare me to serve as CFO (or to support the CFO's duties) within the ministry.

____ *Budget and Financial Management Consulting.* I believe God is calling me to help individuals, families and other organizations learn how to budget and manage their God-given resources in a God-honoring way.

____ *Cost-Effectiveness Analysis of Ministry Programming.* I believe that our ministry is responsible to use its limited resources wisely for maximum ministry impact. I want to support our ministry by conducting a cost-effectiveness analysis to help our leadership plan future ministry strategy.

____ *Steward My Personal Resources for the Sake of the Kingdom.* I believe God has called me to use the resources He has given me wisely and to appropriately invest those resources in the work of ministry.

Teaching

The gift of Teaching is a highly honored spiritual gift within the assembly of Christ-followers, but it is also a gift with severe responsibilities before God. The Bible warns that those who teach among the people will be judged more harshly by God (James 3:1). Spiritually healthy teachers do not simply instruct the minds of their students but first instruct themselves, applying the lessons taught by God through Scripture. Only after they can model the Biblical lesson in their own lives will they be able to authentically teach the lesson to others.

First Corinthians 12:28 lists the gift of Teaching, when applied within the church, as an essential office in the ministry—subservient only to the greater offices of Prophets and Apostles. Ephesians 4:11–14 makes it clear that the teacher's job description includes ". . . to prepare God's people for the works of service." Paul specifically lists Teaching as one of the spiritual gifts in Romans 12:7.

Application

Based upon your personality style, you may prefer applying your gift of Teaching in one or more of the following ways (select all that apply):

____ *Large Group Corporate Instruction.* I believe God would prefer for me to use the teaching gifts He has given me within a large group or congregational setting.

____ *Classroom Instruction.* I believe God would prefer for me to use the teaching gifts He has given me within an adult classroom context.

____ *eLearning Instruction.* I believe God would prefer for me to use the teaching gifts He has given me developing online training programs and providing online instruction and mentorship.

____ *Small Group Instruction.* I believe God would prefer for me to use the teaching gifts He has given me within a small group context of less than twelve people.

____ *Children's Ministries Instructor.* I believe God would prefer for me to use the teaching gifts he has given me within an elementary Biblical education context.

____ *Student Ministries Instructor.* I believe God would prefer for me to use the teaching gifts He has given me within a middle school or high school context.

_____ ***One-On-One Instruction.*** I believe God would prefer for me to use the teaching gifts He has given me within close interpersonal discipling relationships.

Tongues

The gift of Tongues has three purposes within the assembly of Christ-followers:

1.   To be used during periods of prayer, allowing the Holy Spirit to pray through the Christ-follower when he or she does not know how to pray (Rom. 6:26–27);

2.   To receive divine messages from God for the benefit of the assembly of Christ-followers, understanding that someone with the gift of Interpretation of Tongues must be present to interpret (1 Cor. 12:10, 28 and 1 Cor. 14:13–19);

3.   To enable a person to speak an unlearned language for the purposes of evangelism (Acts 2:1–13). In all these formats, the Holy Spirit may choose to use the "tongues of men or angels" (1 Cor. 13:1). The sole purpose of the gift of Tongues is to communicate God's love to others.

Application

Based upon your personality and mix of gifts, you may use your gift of Tongues in any of the following ways (check all that apply):

_____ ***Prayer Language.*** I believe God has called me to a ministry of prayer and so has given me the gift of Tongues to aid me in my prayer ministry.

_____ ***Deliver Divine Messages to the Church.*** I believe God has called me to communicate messages to the body of Christ and has given me the gift of Tongues as the means by which God has chosen to speak through me.

_____ ***Deliver the Gospel to Unlearned Language Groups.*** I believe God has called me to cross-cultural ministry and has given me the gift of Tongues so that I can communicate the gospel to unlearned language groups.

Wisdom

The gift of Wisdom is the special ability given by God to enable a person to "know the right thing to do, and how to do it rightly." When the counsel of a godly person gifted with Wisdom is followed, God is honored, His will is accomplished and the mission of the ministry finds success. Those with the gift of Wisdom may also display the gift of Knowledge. The Apostle Paul identifies the gift of "A Message of Wisdom" among many other spiritual gifts in First Corinthians 12:8. Ephesians 1:17 states: "I keep asking that the God of our Lord Jesus Christ, the glorious Father, may give you the Spirit of wisdom and revelation, so that you may know him better." Colossians 1:9 continues this theme: "For this reason, since the day we heard about you, we have not stopped praying for you and asking God to fill you with the knowledge of his will through all spiritual wisdom and understanding." James 1:5 instructs all Christ-followers: "If any of you lacks wisdom, he should ask God, who gives generously to all without finding fault, and it will be given to him."

Word of Knowledge

The gift of Knowledge is a special insight given by God regarding His will applied to a particular circumstance. The Word of Knowledge given to an individual or to the assembly of Christ-followers will always be supported by the teachings and principles of Scripture. First Corinthians 12:8 identifies the Word of Knowledge among many other spiritual gifts. A dramatic example of the Word of Knowledge in action is found in Acts 5:1–11, where a married couple lied to the Holy Spirit and the church. The Holy Spirit revealed the truth to Peter and disciplined the couple.

This book was produced by CLC Publications. We hope it has been life-changing and has given you a fresh experience of God through the work of the Holy Spirit. CLC Publications is an outreach of CLC Ministries International, a global literature mission with work in over 50 countries. If you would like to know more about us or are interested in opportunities to serve with a faith mission, we invite you to contact us at:

CLC Ministries International
PO Box 1449
Fort Washington, PA 19034

Phone: (215) 542-1242
E-mail: mail@clcusa.org
Website: www.clcusa.org

DO YOU LOVE GOOD CHRISTIAN BOOKS?
Do you have a heart for worldwide missions?

You can receive a FREE subscription to
CLC's newsletter on global literature missions
Order by e-mail at:
clcheartbeat@clcusa.org
or fill in the coupon below and mail to:
P.O. Box 1449
Fort Washington, PA 19034

FREE *HEARTBEAT* SUBSCRIPTION!

Name: _____

Address: _____

_____

Phone: _____ E-mail: _____

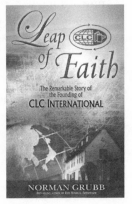

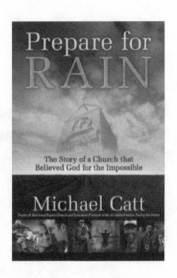

Prepare for Rain

CATT, Michael

The inspiring story of how a church in rural Georgia, no longer content with the status quo, went on to produce a nationally distributed motion picture.

Trade paper • 183 pages
ISBN: 978-0-87508-977-5

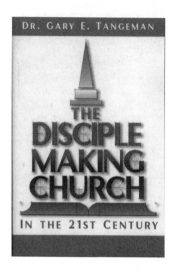

The Disciple-Making Church
in the 21st Century

TANGEMAN, Dr. Gary

What is an effective church? Those responsible for the spiritual development of others will greatly profit from this insightful and practical work on the purpose of the church and the ministry of the believer.

Trade paper • 352 pages
ISBN: 978-0-87508-712-2

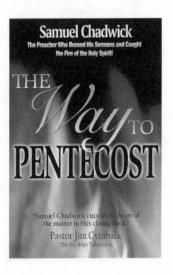

The Way to Pentecost

CHADWICK, Samuel

No other book on the subject of Pentecost so clearly analyzes both our spiritual problems and God's wonderful promise concerning the supply of His Spirit. An excellent choice for those yearning for more of God.

Mass market • 170 pages
ISBN: 978-0-87508-579-1